Food for the Soul

Daily Meditations for Food Addicts

Food Addicts Anonymous

Preface

Welcome to *Food for the Soul.* This daily meditation book was written by food addicts, for food addicts. The following pages offer spiritual stories, visualizations, and meditations to help you in your daily life as you reflect on the experiences of others.

We hope that *Food for the Soul* opens up new avenues of thought for you and inspires you to stay on the path of abstinence and recovery. We are all traveling this road together.

For your convenience, The Twelve Steps, The Twelve Traditions, the FAA Promises and a topic index are included in the back of the book.

Serenity Prayer

*God, grant me the serenity
to accept the things I cannot change,
courage to change the things I can
and the wisdom to know the difference.*

7th Step Prayer

*God, help me listen to my Higher Self as You and I
make the changes in my life that will allow me
to live a free, useful and happy life.
Help me to not find fault with all that I do
and with those who cross my path.
As I continue to stay abstinent,
help me be released from the cravings
for foods that are not in my best interest.
Help me learn that food is to nourish my body so my
spirit can carry out your plans for me.
Help me to be compassionate, trusting, forgiving,
loving and kind to myself and others as
I serve you and the people on earth.
Amen.*

January

February

March

April

May

June

July

August

September

October

November

December

New Year's Day

New Year's is a joyous day of renewal and celebration of the passage of time. It is also, unofficially, National Diet Day. But happily, we recovering food addicts need no longer be caught up in this cycle. New Year's Day is just another day for growth. We may have other resolutions or goals in mind for the new year, but dieting is not among them!

For food addicts still struggling as we enter this new year, this is an opportunity to celebrate by committing to the gift of abstinence, just for today.

Let today be today, and wherever we are in our recovery, may it be a day of freedom from the ravages of food addiction.

For today, I ask God to keep me living fully in the present as I celebrate my abstinence in a new year.

Surrender

Surrender means that I have finally gotten sick and tired of trying to control my eating. How many times did I try to control my food only to end up demoralized and ashamed? How many times would it take before I would be willing to try another way?

Surrender means that I am willing to follow the suggestions of the people with long-term abstinence. I give up the idea of eating sugar, flour, and wheat. I accept completely that I have a powerful biochemical disease.

Surrender means accepting that left untreated, this disease is lethal. It may not kill me physically at first, but it will kill me emotionally and spiritually.

I no longer wish for the day that I can eat addictive foods in moderation. I no longer resent having to spend time preparing meals. I can now look at the positive side of being in recovery from this disease. My meals help to keep my body, mind, and spirit healthy.

Yes, I am powerless over my food addiction. The benefits of admitting this and of living the FAA way are a clear head, excess energy, weight loss, good nutrition, the need for less sleep, and a much better outlook on life!

For today, I ask God for the willingness to surrender.

Wave the White Flag

We admitted we were powerless over our food addiction – that our lives had become unmanageable. (FAA Step One)

I had never admitted powerlessness over anything in my life before finding FAA. Here I was expected to admit I was powerless over sugar, flour, and wheat.

It wasn't until I explored every avenue possible to control my food addiction that I waved the flag of surrender. I had to reach the point of defeat that only those of us who wanted to kill ourselves can understand. I had to take responsibility for the decisions I made and stop blaming others for my life being unmanageable.

I made the choice out of desperation to put down addictive foods and deal with life on life's terms, not as I wanted it to be. The miracle of that decision was being empowered with the skills to manage not only healthy food choices but also to manage my emotions.

In surrendering, I received the gift of life beyond anything I could imagine.

For today, I ask my Higher Power to show me what I need and how I can take care of myself.

Living in the Abstinent Moment

When I was struggling to attain abstinence, my focus was my start date. "I'll start tomorrow." "I'll start Monday." "I'll start on my birthday."

Starting implies continuing. By focusing on a start date, I'm not living in the moment. This approach to abstinence has a subtle but unsettling effect. It keeps me keenly aware of the number of abstinent days behind me.

Today I focus on what is before me – my abstinence right now. I plan and prepare to be abstinent tomorrow. I was abstinent yesterday, but today receives my fullest attention. Today is all that really matters.

I know the approximate date that I got abstinence. Knowing the length of my abstinence is helpful to my fellow food addicts. It gives them some indication of the stability of my abstinence and of where I am in my recovery. I hold it as a minor but important event in my life. What matters to me is that I'm abstinent now.

I need to remain in this moment, living my life and nourishing my body with healthy food at mealtimes. Every day and always, abstinence is a way of life.

For today, I commit to live in the abstinent moment.

Step One Leads Me

Taking Step One, admitting we are powerless over our food addiction, is a great surrender. We can extend that willingness to all areas of life.

Preoccupation with food and unrelenting fear of gaining weight were central to our lives. Letting go of these issues created a space around us, which was perhaps frightening at first, but is now filled with trust and relief that we no longer have to fight endlessly.

Today I seek to turn over to God all that I cannot control. I cannot control world events or other people's actions or attitudes toward me or toward anyone else.

Just for today, I can stay abstinent; I can show up for life. I can strengthen my conscious contact with God through prayer and meditation. I can keep an open mind and continue to learn and grow. I can speak from my heart and love those around me. I can do my best to be gentle and kind to myself and to all who cross my path. I can be who I am today, no more and no less.

For today, I know I am present and aware. I ask God to carry the rest.

Sponsorship

Why do we need a sponsor? Let us count the ways. In food addiction we rationalize the inclusion of certain foods, telling ourselves that they won't harm us. A sponsor is the voice of reason who can help us see clearly that our disease is playing games with us. We honor our sponsor's wisdom regarding the food plan. A sponsor also helps us adapt the FAA food plan to fit our individual needs.

A sponsor supports us and guides us through the cloud of rationalizations into the light of serenity and knowledge. And a sponsor guides us through the Steps of the program. By staying abstinent and working the Steps, we can arrest the disease of food addiction.

We need a sponsor and find a sponsor who has what we want. A sponsor provides the support needed to get through the challenging life events that have the potential to lead us back into addictive eating. As we ourselves become sponsors, we pray to be given the wisdom to guide others effectively. We are grateful for this chain of recovery.

For today, I am grateful that sponsorship exists.

Life on Life's Terms

The renowned psychiatrist Carl Jung said, "Free will is the choice to do gladly that which we must do." If we can accept life on life's terms, then we experience serenity and the joys of everyday life.

This is the ultimate freedom: To choose our reaction to the world around us. Abstinence is the foundation of this freedom. When struggling with addictive foods, we become overwhelmed by depression and negativity. With abstinence it is so much easier to maintain an attitude of gratitude, a spiritual perspective, and joy in our hearts.

But abstinence alone will not render us serene. We must also work the program. Each day, we must make a conscious choice to meet life's challenges and obligations. Rather than seeing the negative in every situation and take blessings for granted, we can build up our gratitude muscles.

Gratitude is a learned skill that takes daily practice. With the gift of abstinence, we can choose to be positive, to focus on the blessings in our lives, and to welcome happiness. This is freedom.

For today, I ask God to grant me the willingness to gladly embrace life on life's terms.

Changing Faulty Thinking

It is humbling to admit that we are powerless when for so long we believed we had control. We clung to the fantasy that we had great influence on the affairs of our life. We may have believed that if we just tried harder, worked longer, found a new method, or changed circumstances, then we would succeed. Disengaging from these beliefs can be especially difficult if we have experienced some success, which fed our drive for utter control.

We come to a point of surrender, of recognizing that our disease of food addiction is completely beyond our control. We are truly powerless over our addiction. But we have found a solution – to humbly surrender to the process of recovery.

As we grow in recovery, we begin to perceive our powerlessness over events, people, and circumstances. We learn to control our attitudes, our words, and our actions. We choose to align our will with God's will for us. This wisdom is our greatest power. We are lifted out of the futile struggle and misery of addiction. We live a simple and serene life. We are free.

For today, I ask for God's guidance, and then I listen humbly for the answers.

Facing Relapse

Relapse may be a frightening word for some recovering food addicts. Through our own or a fellow member's experience, we know that the duration of a relapse can last from a few hours to a few years. And some people never find their way back to the FAA rooms. We may once again find ourselves falling into a black pit, forgetting the lessons that we learned in recovery.

A relapse brings home what we hear at meetings. We hear from other members that the warning signs of a relapse may include attending fewer meetings or giving up service positions. It may include being dishonest with our sponsor or shutting off our connection with our Higher Power. Ultimately, in relapse, we pick up sugar, flour, and wheat. We are then once again faced with the truth that relapse is progressive in nature.

We do not need to be insecure about our abstinence. Abstinence and the joys that it brings are ours to keep. With loving, attentive care, the gift of abstinence can be ours forever, one day at a time.

For today, I ask God to keep me from denial of the signs of relapse.

From Fear to Faith

For many of us, fear of getting or staying fat was the primary motivator for much of our early abstinence, and it may continue to motivate some of us. We have come to see, however, that belief in a Power greater than ourselves – not fear – is the true foundation of our abstinence.

When we are connected to our Higher Power through prayer, meditation, gratitude, and living in the moment, then we find recovery. We no longer binge to the point of semi-consciousness. We are not besieged by endless anxiety or by the profound depression that in the past would have led us back into the food or for some, would have led us back into restricting food.

We do not need to block out life. We do not wish to return to the days of food-induced obliteration. We enjoy the moment, even the challenging ones, because we have God by our side, reassuring us that we are learning and living.

Abstinence is much more easily sustained through faith in the process of recovery rather than through fear. Our disease has no power when we continue to make conscious contact with the God of our understanding.

For today, I pray that I place my faith in the process of recovery.

Analysis Paralysis

We food addicts have a way of overanalyzing everything. All of this thinking interferes with living, leaving us with a classic case of analysis paralysis. In addiction, we did not realize that obsessing over every detail of daily life is not necessary or productive.

In recovery, we realize that we were incessantly worried and chronically stressed, and these character defects posed a threat to our continued abstinence. In abstinence, we let go of extraneous speculation and worry. After all, worrying does not help to keep the plane up in the air!

The Serenity Prayer is a wonderful, immediate tool that offers guidance when we find ourselves fretting over something. We first ask God for the wisdom to know whether we can change the situation. If so, we ask for the courage to make the change and then move into action. If we cannot change the situation, we ask for the serenity to accept it as it is.

Stress for us is no longer chronic. We address it with action or we let it go.

For today, I can say the Serenity Prayer to relieve stressful moments.

Resentment

What is resentment? The dictionary defines it as anger at something unworthy, unjust, or mean. As we work the Twelve Steps of FAA, we become aware of how resentment manifests in our lives.

Before we had the tools of the program, we may have unknowingly set ourselves up for disappointment and failure. We may have offered to do something for someone that we really didn't want to do and then justified our anger.

Today we offer our help only if it's something we really want to do. We no longer have a need to do things for others just so people will like us. Nor do we expect favors in return.

We are learning to accept and trust ourselves and not to depend on others for our happiness. It's good to be aware of our feelings and not let them consume us. Best of all, we don't have to eat over resentments.

For today, I ask God to help me let go of resentments and to stay abstinent.

Responses of Recovery

Today my ability to respond is much different than it was in the past. I know that the only things I have power over are my actions, attitudes, and feelings.

I respond to my disease by following my food plan and by weighing, measuring, and committing my food. I also pray, meditate, write, read, work the Steps, sponsor, and give service.

I respond to my addiction by attending meetings, staying abstinent, consulting with my Higher Power, and acknowledging my powerlessness on a daily basis.

I respond to life by listening, living one day at a time, and asking for guidance from fellow recovering food addicts and from my Higher Power.

I may tend to react addictively to life's events, but as I progress in recovery, I am learning a new way to respond to people, places, and things. I am learning to stop before I act. I am learning how to be more open and honest about who I am and what I want. Only by the grace of God are these miracles happening.

When things don't go my way or as I expected them to go, I accept what I can't change and ask God to show me how to change what I can. When I am faced with disappointment, I can respond with prayer and open myself to a power greater than me.

For today, I use my recovery tools and reap the miracles that follow.

Leave Yesterday in the Past

I have a past, but I don't have to live there anymore. With abstinence, I no longer have to rehash my regrets. Resentments and anger that caused me pain can be released to the universe and to the welcoming arms of my Higher Power.

With abstinence and the Twelve Steps, I have today and a future that is bright even on a rainy day. Abstinence and my recovery tools give me the clarity to make choices that are good for me, to love myself, and to draw closer to my Higher Power. I still will make mistakes – I am human after all. Now, though, I can make amends. I can pray for those with whom I disagree. I can remember to ask my Higher Power to *bless them, change me.* And I can cherish the joy of living in today.

Living in recovery is not geared so much to reliving the past as to finding appropriate attitudes for living this particular day successfully.

For today, I release the resentments of yesterday and live in the joy of the present.

Slow Down and Listen

For some of us, prayer comes easily but meditation takes more practice. We may find it difficult to stay in the present, which is what meditation is all about. Our minds wander. They slip out of the present. We find ourselves reminiscing about the past and fantasizing about the future. If we're distressed, we anticipate the pain to come or remember the pain that happened last time.

When we become aware that we have wandered from the present, we can ask our Higher Power to bring us back. We can gently let go of extraneous thoughts and let ourselves concentrate on our breathing, on a single word, or on a flame flickering. We can ask our Higher Power to help us stay in today.

For today, I take the time to pray and meditate.

A Precious Gift

My abstinence is a gift from my Higher Power. It did not come to me through wishing or willpower. On the contrary, I failed utterly in all my attempts to get abstinent. But once I surrendered, I saw that it had always been freely offered, held out to me by loving hands. I simply had to accept it.

Abstinence is a gift, but it is not magic. I had to do the footwork before I was open to receiving this gift, and I continue with this work to keep my abstinence. Like every other food addict in recovery, I am only one bite away from tumbling back into the abyss of addictive eating.

Each morning I pray. I thank God for keeping me abstinent during the preceding 24 hours, and I earnestly ask that God keep me abstinent for yet another day. I weigh and measure my food. I work the Steps. I reach out to others for strength, and I do service.

I cherish my abstinence, knowing that it is easier to stay abstinent than get abstinent.

For today, I treasure this precious gift of abstinence and take the steps necessary to keep it.

Strength in Unity

Our common welfare should come first; personal recovery depends on FAA unity. (FAA Tradition One)

After spending years feeling alone and different from everyone else, I finally found solace in the words of the first Tradition, particularly in the word *unity*. Tradition One declares our unity of purpose. We are bound together by a common illness and we have a common path of recovery. Our common welfare depends on each of us.

An informed group conscience keeps our meetings on target so that we can be of the greatest help to newcomers and old-timers alike. When the group is unified in purpose, with its eyes on the welfare of all, each individual in that group can be helped. Unity can be seen as the theme that runs through all the Traditions. Our love for one another and our singleness of purpose allows us to stand firm in the face of an ever-changing world. Unity helps us as individuals and lends integrity to the fellowship.

For today, I cherish FAA's oneness of purpose and focus on the need for unity.

I'm Grateful

For years I tried to recover from my food problem but could not because I did not understand how addictive substances poisoned every area of my life. Even after learning about food addiction, I kept a tight grip on my sugar, flour, and wheat. Sure, I wanted to be thin, free of food obsession, and happy. I just wanted to have all of those things without having to make any changes.

It took years of pain and suffering for me to get to the point where I realized that I could not have my cake and sanity too. I became so miserable that nothing else worked. The FAA program offered me what I knew was my last chance! There is no place else for me to go.

Our program is for those of us who desperately want recovery. It is not magic, but it is magical.

For today, I openly express my gratitude for Food Addicts Anonymous.

The Miracle of Recovery

How did this miracle of recovery happen for me? Perhaps it all started when I realized that God wanted to show me a way out of addiction. I used to think that my weight was too unimportant to bring to God. Now I know that nothing is too small for God to heal.

Food addiction is not too small a thing to talk to God about. This disease affects every area of my life, and I am powerless over it. I need to tap into a Higher Power to stay in recovery. Talking to and sharing my heart with my Higher Power is an extremely important tool for spiritual growth.

I can talk to God by writing a dialog. I tell God what my worries are, and then I write what I think a loving God would tell me. I can write my Step One this way and, indeed, every Step this way. This type of writing allows me to see and to accept that my life was unmanageable before FAA and that I could not control my behavior while eating addictive foods.

I ask for help to understand the true meaning of powerlessness. Powerlessness does not mean hopelessness. Accepting reality, surrendering denial, and following the program means that I am giving myself to my Higher Power for healing.

For today, I talk to God and in return am given the strength to stay abstinent.

Our Primary Purpose

To recover from the disease of food addiction I abstain from sugar, flour, wheat, and other high carbohydrate foods. I work the Steps, with the guidance of a sponsor and find a power greater than myself, in order to stay abstinent.

The program tells me if I keep the gifts I have received to myself, I am likely to lose them. To keep my abstinence and recovery, I must share my experience, strength, and hope with other food addicts so that they can achieve abstinence as well.

This is a *we* program. I can't achieve abstinence without your help. I want to remember that our primary purpose is to stay abstinent and help other food addicts achieve abstinence. What a humbling experience to admit that I can't do this alone, and what a relief to know that I will never be alone again. The fellowship of FAA is powerful.

For today, I give it away so that I can keep it.

Changing My World

The remarkable thing about Step One is that although it is the most difficult step for many members, it can be the most rewarding. Step One is the pathway to personal freedom, growth, and recovery.

Once I surrendered totally to being powerless over my food addiction, I was able to focus on my life, to blossom and be happy.

I've wasted time and energy trying to control my weight. I brooded. I would explode at my partner in fury when my clothes did not fit. Hours of precious life were wasted.

When I finally took Step One and was freed from the obsession of eating sugar, flour, and wheat, I was free to make changes in my thinking and my attitudes toward the world. Gradually, I became joyful in realizing that my world had changed because I had changed.

For today, I continue to work the Steps in order to blossom into what God wants me to be.

Today Is a New Day

Today is a new day, and anything is possible. Today I will eat healthy food, surround myself with healthy people, and use my gifts and creativity for a greater good. I will help one person today, even if it is only in example or by lending my ear.

My abstinence gives me balance in my life. I don't want to forget how horrible it was to be in active food addiction and how it hurt those around me.

By attending an FAA meeting, I share my experiences with those who have found this wonderful path and FAA fellowship. On my way home, I pray that others will be led here by their Higher Power. I am grateful for the continued growth of all those in this program who have walked before me and are showing me the way.

For today, I rejoice in knowing that I am blessed with knowledge of my disease and that I can live in the solution.

Getting to Step Zero

Before we came to FAA, we may not have had the desire to stop eating addictive foods. None of us ever wanted to give up sugar, flour, and wheat. We only wanted to be a normal weight and to have a normal relationship with food, free of our shame about our bodies and our eating habits. If there were an easier way, we would have found it. We tried many routes, including diet clubs, weight loss centers, exercising, other Twelve Step programs, hospitalizations, and surgeries. All of these efforts failed.

In the midst of our despair, our Higher Power guided us to the program of FAA. We learned that we needed only the desire to stop eating addictively to begin our recovery journey. If we did not have the desire, we asked our Higher Power to help us. We attended meetings and listened to others who had what we wanted, and eventually the desire for recovery overcame the desire to do it our way. We become willing to go to any lengths to be relieved of the cravings for foods that are not in our best interest.

For today, I pray for the desire and willingness to abstain from eating sugar, flour, and wheat.

Facing Temptation

Temptation is everywhere. We pass giant billboards along the highway that promote sugary foods. We view stylized photos of desserts in magazines and TV commercials that urge us to treat ourselves with sugar. We visit a friend and see a sugary breakfast cereal on her kitchen counter or smell fresh-baked cookies as we pass the bakery in the strip mall. Temptation is everywhere, but so is our Higher Power.

If our abstinence feels shaky and we question whether it is really worth it to resist temptation, we can always call on our Higher Power for help and support. We might ask, "God, please relieve me from cravings for those foods that are not in my best interest. Please remind me that nothing tastes as sweet as the freedom from obsession over sugar, flour, and wheat. Please bless me with the precious gift of abstinence for another 24 hours." It is amazing how strong we can become when we ask our Higher Power for help.

For today, I ask my Higher Power to lift my obsessions and fill me with the strength to continue my abstinence, which is the sweetest gift of all.

Similarities, Not Differences

Sometimes my ego tells me that I am different than everyone else in the program, perhaps because of my sex, my appearance, my background, or my belief that I am not as sick as others.

I can choose to focus on the differences between us or I can listen to what other members have to say. When I listen, I find that we are all very much alike when it comes to our food addiction and the way it has ravaged our lives.

I cannot consider myself different in FAA. If I do, I isolate myself from others and from contact with my Higher Power. If I feel isolated in FAA, it is not something for which others are responsible. I alone am responsible for seeking out our similarities and embracing our differences.

The ability for one food addict to identify with another food addict is the music of this spiritual program.

For today, I focus on our similarities rather than our differences.

Focused, Directed and Free

In recovery, we relinquish much of our perceived power. We accept our powerlessness over our addiction and turn our will and our lives over to the care of our Higher Power.

As recovery progresses, the powers we actually possess become clearer. We have the power to show up for life, to choose our attitude, and to react or not react to people and circumstances.

We have the power to be present, to remain aware, to make choices with a clear head, and to go with the flow.

We have the power to perceive and fulfill God's will.

No longer distracted by a need to control that which we could never control anyway, nor cleaning up the chaos such attempts created, we are now free to focus our energies on living in today. Where we were frustrated generalists before, frazzled and spread too thin, we can now specialize and come to excel in the fine art of living, loving, and experiencing the joys of being alive, one day at a time.

For today I make the choice to stay in recovery so that I may be present, alert, and free to do God's will.

Don't Play With Fire

With spiritual fitness comes the gift of enjoying social interaction and focusing on life, not food. Our goal becomes going out into the world, not hiding in our homes with the curtains drawn, the TV on, and the refrigerator open.

To maintain our abstinence, we must be honest about our own sensitivities. If bakeries still call our name, if pizza parlors are still seductive, if family get-togethers revolve around food, then we probably have no business being there. We strive to protect ourselves from dangerous situations.

No matter how much abstinent time we have and no matter how committed we are to abstaining from sugar, flour, and wheat, we find that it is best to avoid situations where we might give in to the disease. We can ask a guest to purchase and serve the birthday cake. We can excuse ourselves when friends serve dessert at a dinner party and instead help with the dishes. We can go grocery shopping after we have eaten a meal so that we are not hungry. Most importantly, we can examine our motives for putting ourselves in a dangerous situation.

For today, I do whatever it takes to avoid situations where I may be tempted to break my abstinence.

Nourishment or Nurturing?

Food is designed to nourish. As a food addict, I have warped food's purpose from one of nourishment to one of nurturing. In the disease, I have looked to food to give me comfort, solace, love, and strength. I have sought answers in food that aren't there.

Food addiction is but a symptom of my problem. Yes, I am a food addict, and my default mode is to turn to food, eating, restricting, or attempts at weight control to try to fix a problem or stop a feeling. My problem is spiritual in nature. In essence, I forget God. I forget to pray and to listen. I forget that God is all-powerful and has all the answers. Instead, I am doubtful and I believe that I am alone.

Today I know I am not alone. God, along with loving, wonderful recovering food addicts who share the solution surround me. They guide me, console me, and share with me their experience, strength, and hope. They, along with my willingness to live this program, are what make my recovery work.

For today, I believe that no matter how I do it, reaching out to God and to other recovering food addicts helps me stay in recovery.

Building a Solid Foundation

Step One may seem easy: All we have to do is admit that we have a problem. However, if we want to move forward in our recovery, we must find the deeper meaning of Step One.

We must look at all the ways in which we are powerless over our food addiction. Did we binge despite the fact that it was ruining our lives and the lives of those who care about us? Did we endanger ourselves or others to get our *fix*? Did our binge foods become our primary purpose?

How about the ways in which our lives had become unmanageable? Were we disappointing our family? Our friends? Our employers? Were we jeopardizing our livelihood or our relationships with loved ones? Were we emotionally present for anyone?

At an even deeper level, did we come to see that our food addiction was continually breaking our hearts?

It is important that we take the time to explore all of the implications of Step One. After all, Step One is the foundation step. Without a good foundation, we can't build on our recovery. Seeing who we really are when we are active in our food addiction is a solid foundation on which to build our program.

For today, I continue to take Step One to keep my foundation solid.

Ego Versus God's Will

In recovery, I have discovered my body knows many things that my mind is sometimes too stubborn to accept. My ego leads me astray by persuading me that my willpower is enough to keep me out of the sugar, flour, and wheat. Ice cream starts looking like the solution to all my problems instead of the descent into madness it truly is. Then the battle begins, me against the disease, duking it out inside the walls of my denial. The physical signs of severe tension capture my attention and I start to wonder what is causing the knots in my stomach and back. Solitude and attention directed inward allows the players in this battle to surface.

My ego endangers my recovery by trying to persuade me that my will is better for me than God's will is, but my body knows the truth. Turning my will over to my Higher Power, surrendering the battle, and picking up the tools of the FAA program restore my serenity and ease my tension.

For today, I enlist the help of my Higher Power and take the time to listen to my body's signals.

The Action of Surrender

After years of struggling to surrender, I realized that surrender is an action word. The simplest definition of surrender for me today is to follow my food plan exactly as written. I have spent years trying to make the food plan conform to my will. I could talk about surrender, cry about surrender, and pray about surrender, but in the end, I just had to do it! What freedom there is in this surrender.

I will continue to surrender as long as I continue to do the First Step. I need to continually recognize that I am powerless over this addiction. I need to always remember how unmanageable my life is when I eat addictively. I know I am much more willing to resign from the debating team today. I am willing to take direction. I have been warned about giving power to the disease.

When I follow the food plan, I no longer have to obsess about what I am going to eat, and I find that there are many hours left in the day for living.

For today, I surrender my will and experience the freedom from my obsession with food.

Accepting Guidance

Came to believe that a Power greater than ourselves could restore us to sanity. (FAA Step Two)

I am grateful that what I have done in the past to try to control my eating has humbly brought me to Food Addicts Anonymous. Everything else I tried failed, and now I have the gift of abstinence. I just had to admit I needed help. For today, I am ready to admit that I need help and guidance not only from the fellowship, but also from a Higher Power.

Today I do not pick up no matter what. There may be times today when I crave foods that are harmful to me. The answer is not in the food. There may be times today that I feel lonely and isolated. Another bite will not help. When these negative feelings are aroused in me, I now know that I can turn to the fellowship and my Higher Power. With the FAA fellowship on one side of me and a Higher Power on the other, I am protected, comforted, and supported throughout this day.

For today, I reach out to my Higher Power and other recovering food addicts.

Open Your Fist and Let Go

A little boy's favorite toy truck broke. Crying, he took it to his father and held it up. His father saw that the front axle had come loose; it would be simple to fix. He reached for the truck. The little boy was so upset, though, that he held onto it tightly. He imagined that perhaps his father would throw the broken toy away. His father gently chuckled, "We'll have your truck good as new in a second, but first you have to let it go."

Letting go is an act of surrender. Whether we are struggling with the food or with another issue, we must learn to trust our Higher Power. We cannot be given something better if we refuse to let go of what we have.

If we find that we need help but resist letting go of worry and futile attempts at control, we can incorporate into our prayers this simple gesture:

Hold up your closed hand, palm up. Imagine that you are holding your trouble within your closed fist. As you say, "Higher Power, please take this from me," open your hand. Visualize the problem being taken from you.

It is no longer yours – you have surrendered it.

For today, I thank God for taking that which I surrender.

This Twenty-Four Hours

The 24-hour program is a phrase used to describe a basic FAA approach to the challenge of staying abstinent. We never swear off sugar, flour, and wheat for life. We never take pledges committing ourselves to refrain from bingeing tomorrow.

We recognize that our greatest challenge is to stay abstinent right now! This moment is the only one that we have. Yesterday is gone. Tomorrow never comes.

We can start a new day at dawn, or we might begin a new day in the middle or even at the end of the day. When we accept the truth about our addiction to sugar, flour, and wheat, we are given the courage to accept abstinence and renew our lives at any given moment. History no longer determines our fate. With God and the program in hand, we can write a new story.

Let this new story be one of recovery. This new story may differ from any experiences we have had. It may feel awkward at first. But with the loving support of the fellowship, living an abstinent life will soon become second nature.

Whether we are new to recovery or an old-timer, we pray that we accept the gift of abstinence each moment of each day.

For today, I focus on the present, not on the past or the future.

Life's Basic Lessons

Being in the food is playing hooky from the school of life. During those years of addictive eating, we simply were not showing up for many of the basic lessons: how to take care of ourselves, how to be available to others, how to make small talk and socialize, how to run an orderly household, how to relax, how to have fun. We were zoned out and stumbling along. No wonder life grew unmanageable.

Today we are learning many of these things. Each time we choose abstinence over the food, we are showing up for the lessons God has been trying to teach us all these years. As long as we remember to let go of any sense of shame for being a little behind in life's lessons, we can enjoy learning to live. We enjoy the process, and the reward – a manageable, serene, and beautiful life. May those days of truancy be past, and may there be many days of learning ahead.

For today, I will show up for life.

With Recovery Comes Sanity

Came to believe that a Power greater than ourselves could restore us to sanity. (FAA Step Two)

In order to take Step Two, we begin to recognize just how sick our relationship was with sugar, flour and wheat. We admitted that our lives were unmanageable, but were we really insane? Perhaps not certifiably so. We managed to function at a certain level in life, but our ability to maintain appearances was in marked contrast to our insane behavior around food. Was it sane to endanger our lives by bingeing, purging or starving ourselves? Was it sane to resolve each day not to repeat our destructive ways, and then to do so with absolute abandon repeatedly?

This was a hard way to live. In recovery, we want sanity; we want to behave sanely around food. We have to believe that healing is possible. Even if we struggle with this Step, we can act "as if." We do the footwork. We abstain from addictive foods. We work the program. We learn to rely on God to keep us abstinent and to help us heal.

Slowly, we came to believe that God could and would restore us to sanity.

For today, I trust that God will direct me and keep me sane.

Reaching Out

Nothing increases my chances of staying abstinent and in recovery more than reaching out to another food addict in need. There is a magical connection when one food addict extends a helping hand to another. This is the basis of our wonderful Twelve Step fellowship.

We speak the same language. We have walked the same path.

By reaching out, I am putting into motion one of the spiritual truths of FAA – it's in giving that I receive.

There is another benefit from the practice of reaching out. I have the unique opportunity of watching these food addicts get abstinent and begin to thrive. Then they, in return, can begin reaching out to others. Maybe one day I will be in need and they will reach out to me. This is how our fellowship comes full circle.

For today, I will reach out to another food addict. It is in this way that I help keep the lifeline of recovery open.

Courage To Love

Ultimately, the deep sense of emptiness that pervades the food addict's soul is a spiritual void. In recovery, we connect with God in part through loving relationships with our fellow human beings. We need to relate meaningfully with others, lest loneliness leave us vulnerable to the call of addictive foods.

Intimacy, which involves letting others get close, can be frightening. However, through abstinence in our recovery program, we become willing to tolerate feeling vulnerable, and we can accept the risk of rejection, loss, and criticism.

Courage to venture into relationships comes from a strong sense of self. If we love and accept ourselves absolutely, exactly as we are, then we will not internalize any negative judgments that we may receive from others. In fact, negative feedback can be a blessing. If we can calmly consider another person's criticism and find it to be true, then we can change. If, on the other hand, we find the criticism to be unfounded, then we learn to let it go. We develop a secure sense of self. We know what to take on and what to let slide. We grow in wisdom.

For today, I ask God to give me the courage to connect spiritually with others.

Using Energy For Good

Before FAA, I would eat voraciously or devour greedily. That's how I got through life. I ate my binge foods with greed and haste. I blasted my way through the day without enjoying each precious moment. Perhaps it was because I thought there would never be enough. Or I wasn't enough.

I know today in recovery that when I devour my meals, I can't be present to savor the blessings that surround me. Instead, bingeing numbs me and causes me to miss experiences that will never come my way again.

Today I want to approach life voraciously. I want only what is good for my body, mind and spirit, and I want to soak up everything that I can in recovery. I know that I will have enough and that I am enough.

For today, I ask for the grace to look at my eating history with honesty and compassion.

Just Say No

Today I will follow the suggested food plan. When I do this, my life is centered and balanced. My disease may try to convince me to pick up sugar, flour, or wheat. It might tempt me, berate me, or argue with me. It may try flattery, telling me how deserving I am of a reward.

Hard-earned lessons have taught me to recognize and dismiss this treacherous voice. If I choose to listen to the disease, it will destroy me. Recovery graces me with a healthy mind as well as a healthy body. I have developed the mental muscle to say no to the disease. I have learned to take care of myself.

While in the disease, I was a prisoner. In recovery, I am free.

For today, I ask God to give me the wisdom to recognize destructive voices and the courage to deny them an audience.

A Three-Legged Stool

Physical recovery, which involves ridding my body of addictive substances, must come before I can begin to heal emotionally and spiritually. Recovery in FAA is progressive. We continue to grow and develop throughout our lives. We do not graduate from this program. Instead, we get to higher levels of awareness.

We can choose to follow the spiritual principles outlined in the Twelve Steps, which contribute to our emotional healing, or we can go back to addictive foods and escape reality.

If I do not work on all three legs of the recovery stool – physical, emotional, and spiritual recovery – then I will fall. Balance is the key. If I work the Steps, continue to surrender to a Higher Power, and abstain from addictive substances, I will recover one day at a time.

For today, I follow the spiritual principles of recovery to help me maintain balance in my life.

Accepting the Disease of Food Addiction

Acceptance is a good place to be.

In my early FAA days, although I'd eat the food suggested, the quantity was out of control, my weight gradually crept up, my serenity diminished, and my old fears returned. I had to accept that my life would be lost if I was not willing to plan, report, and follow through on my commitment to eat only what is on my food plan for today.

Today I am in full acceptance of the actions required. I keep my food squeaky clean. I know that *A Guide to Abstinence* works. The weighing and measuring, the FAA Steps, Traditions and tools have become an integral part of how I live. This God-given program works when I surrender and accept FAA in its entirety.

This is a simple program for complicated people. It is a program for those who want it, not for those who need it. I want it and choose to follow the program one day at a time, reaping all the abundance that recovery offers me.

For today, I accept myself as I am – a person with a disease trying to get healthy and sane.

Knowing My True Self

Excessive attachment to physical appearance mars serenity. It is a gift and a pleasure to look and feel attractive. But it is an infinite well of discontentment to measure self-worth by this standard. Doing so may leave us feeling that we are not enough.

To judge myself by my physical appearance is as absurd as judging myself by my material possessions. Would a beautiful new car render me a superior person? If the car got dented, would my self-esteem plummet? I might want the car to be in good shape so that it will run well and have a pleasing appearance, but I wouldn't base my worth as a human being on these superficial values.

It is the same with my body. I want to look attractive and be healthy, because beauty is a pleasure and health is a joy. But my shimmering spirit, which lies within, is my real essence. It remains pristine and untouched by my outward appearance. I am God's child: beautiful, loved, and precious. Nothing can alter that.

As acceptance and knowledge of my true spirit emerges, my sense of self strengthens. When self-doubt arises, I pause to remember who I really am, and God reassures me that I am enough and so much more.

For today, I pray for ever-deepening knowledge of my true self.

Guidance for the Day

Rather than do it our way, we ask this Higher Power for guidance, for help to find the way. (<u>Food Addicts Anonymous</u>, *Some Thoughts on Spirituality*)

I know I cannot do this alone. I know that many times my actions have netted unhappy results, because I chose to go it alone. In recovery, I am learning to rely on a power greater than myself to guide my actions, in order to avoid the same pitfalls.

Just for today, I listen to the suggestions of recovering people. My Higher Power speaks through other people to get the message of recovery to me.

I pray that my Higher Power's will be done through me.

I meditate and listen for God's voice.

I trust my intuition. Intuition is the voice of my Higher Power within me.

I venture out of isolation. I reach out and make contact with another recovering addict so that I can hear the voice of recovery speaking.

For today, I look for ways to recognize and follow the guidance given me by my Higher Power.

Sweeter Still

Today is the day we call Valentine's Day and we celebrate the love of the people we have in our lives. Before coming to FAA, I didn't celebrate love on this day. I celebrated one of the days when society sanctions mounds of chocolates and candy. It was a day when I could buy an entire pound of candy and not be embarrassed that it was too much, or have anyone become suspicious that I bought it only for myself. It was a day I could openly binge without anyone commenting on my lack of control.

With abstinence and recovery, I now cherish Valentine's Day. What a gift love is in my life – the gift of love I receive from the Higher Power – unconditional – the only place I can ever expect or receive unconditional love. The gift of love from my program friends who support me in my abstinence. The selfless gift of love from my sponsor – without whom this journey would be very different.

My mind is clearer, my heart is filled with more love, the people around me have more of my attention and I am more positive and appreciative. I no longer wait for this day on the calendar to celebrate the love in my life.

For today, I cherish the love of those around me and freely give my own love.

The Ultimate Authority

For our group purpose there is but one ultimate authority – a loving God as God is expressed in our group conscience. Our leaders are but trusted servants; they do not govern. (FAA Tradition Two)

In making decisions and discussing possible changes in FAA, we can too easily fall prey to the "my way or the highway" attitude. Perhaps those very situations present themselves to remind us that we are in need of an attitude adjustment. Whenever we are considering any change in our group, we can only be assured of a blessed outcome when each of us is sincerely submitting ourselves to our Higher Power's guidance.

Abstinence is not the only gift of love we receive from God. This "loving God as God is expressed" seeks to bless us all individually and as a group. Opinions filled with me's, I's and my's indicate that we are being led by our egos. It has been said that the word *ego* stands for "easing God out." It is vital to the abstinence of every member of FAA that we seek our ultimate authority's guidance in all of our affairs.

For today, I seek God's guidance and will for my own life and the life of FAA as a whole.

Abstinence Is My Priority

The definition of insanity is doing the same thing over and over and expecting different results. To get new results, I found that I had to become willing to learn to do things differently. Abstinence is now my priority. I had to eliminate anything in my life that could threaten my abstinence.

The meaningful things in my life today are only possible through abstinence. I am unwilling to risk losing these things by giving anything more importance. Sometimes this means making difficult choices to let go of some people, places or things.

Everything good in my life today is a result of abstinence. Making abstinence my number one priority is not fanaticism; it's truly life and death for me. It's just that simple.

For today, I make abstinence my number one priority.

Submission is Not Surrender

Submission is doing what I have to do until I get to my goal or destination, and then I'll be able to quit. Surrender is giving myself up to another power. Surrender is absolute knowledge that my denial and grandiosity aren't working.

Whenever I have submitted to a diet or to anything else in my life, I always had a plan of what I'd do when I get what I really want. But when I found out what true surrender was and really surrendered, I let go of all my preconceived notions.

Many of my ways were distorted and twisted from this disease. The disease does that: it twists and turns things until I think I know everything and can handle it myself.

Surrender, for me, means admitting that I can't do this myself and I don't know everything. I surrender by working this program with all of its tools. I surrender by doing things that are opposite of what I would normally do: making phone calls when I don't want to, exercising when I don't feel like it, following the food plan when I want something else.

I listen to the experience of those who have gone before me and I follow in their footsteps.

For today, I am thankful that I am willing to surrender.

Abstinent Gratification

Sometimes when I am dealing with something difficult, I find myself falling into the old, habitual patterns by wanting to binge. It is in such instances that I am reminded once again of my powerlessness. Through the grace of God, I choose short-term discomfort of life for the long-term comfort of abstinence.

I now realize that reaching for food is an immature response – a young child wanting instant gratification for comfort. Instead, I can strengthen my recovery through meditation, prayer, and seeking my Higher Power for guidance. I have learned to ask myself, "What am I feeling?" and "What do I need?" I can meet these needs with alternatives to bingeing, such as journaling, resting, talking with friends, and walking outdoors. I can grow up and be a mature adult and nurture myself by learning to give myself what I truly need.

For today, I trust that with God I have everything I need.

Willingness Is Not a Permanent Condition

Very few things in life are permanent. We are not happy every day, nor are we always sad, lazy, energetic, or angry. Willingness is not a permanent condition, either. Though we may come through the doors of FAA with absolute willingness to do whatever it takes to be relieved of our addiction, over time our resolve may weaken. Perhaps we start to feel resentful that we can't eat like "normal" people. Perhaps the excitement of early abstinence passes. Perhaps we've let ourselves forget the pain and suffering of our last binge. Feeling our willingness weaken is a red flag to use our tools more.

We can pray for the willingness to be willing. We can look back to the earliest writings in our journals to remind ourselves of the despair we felt when we were bingeing or starving. We can reach out to others at meetings and one-on-one. We can thank our Higher Power every night for the willingness we had today. Like abstinence, willingness is a gift to be treasured and never taken for granted.

For today, I ask God to grant me the willingness to go to any lengths to stay abstinent.

Unblocking Happiness

While recovering in another fellowship, I observed others as being so happy. I often wondered why the same wasn't true for me.

After coming into the rooms of Food Addicts Anonymous, I was able to see that as long as I was eating addictively, I was blocking happiness.

I learned here that food addiction is a biochemical disease and that when I picked up that first bite, my chances at happiness were limited. I would be unable to think or act clearly and happiness would elude me. My life was unmanageable.

Once I became abstinent from addictive foods, and by working the Twelve Steps, I was able to deal with my low self-image. It is amazing to be able to accept myself just as I am. In recovery, I am able to recognize the good around me. I now have a long gratitude list and feel genuinely happy.

For today, I wear a smile and I focus on gratitude for this life-changing program.

Reaching Out

If I had not been born a food addict, I might not have had a reason to seek God. I knew I was insane around food and in my relationships. Nonetheless, I had a problem coming to believe that a power greater than myself could restore me to sanity. Is God really bigger than my food addiction?

As I began to pray to change, I got the message that God restores us to sanity through the help of others. This does not mean that we must take what others say as the final word. However, we find that in connecting with others we are relieved of our insanity on a daily basis. Every day we can reach out to another food addict, talk about our insanity, and find relief.

Perhaps we are food addicts so that we can draw closer to God. With God's help, we remain abstinent and carry the message to the still-suffering food addict.

For today, I remember that when I feel the insanity of the disease of food addiction, relief is only a prayer and a phone call away.

Praying for a Sponsor

Some of us may have once believed that we did not need a sponsor. All we had to do was follow the FAA food plan, which soon turned into the "my way" food plan. Our disease begins to minimize all the changes and modifications that we make. We may hear in our heads such rationalizations as, "So what if you're not following the food plan exactly. You're still eating so much better than you were before."

In time, we become dissatisfied with our own way. We want the kind of recovery described by our old-timers. We hear them say that abstinence is the highest form of self-love. Perhaps for the first time in our lives, we do not want to settle. We want to experience squeaky-clean abstinence. It is then that we realize that we really do need the guidance of a sponsor.

As we frequent meetings, we may look at every other food addict in the room and ask ourselves, "What about that one? Is that person the one?" If we keep asking our Higher Power for help, we find that we are given direction. We are given the sponsor whom we were meant to encounter at that particular time in our lives.

The wisdom that we gain from our sponsors gives us hope and courage.

For today, I follow the directions given to me by my sponsor.

Some Concepts Must be the Same

What is your concept of God? Step Two says we "came to believe that a Power greater than ourselves could restore us to sanity."

The FAA literature suggests, "We must believe that God is loving, accepting, and healing." Our first step in the journey toward belief in a Higher Power may be in simply being willing to consider that a Higher Power exists for us.

Second, we come to believe that God loves. This love means that God will never let go of us in the highs and lows, in the calm and in the storm, in joy and in grief, or when we believe and when we doubt.

Third, we come to believe that God accepts. God does not say "I'll love you if…" or "I'll love you when…." Therefore, I don't have to get my act together or become perfect. God is ready and willing to help me no matter what shape I'm in.

Fourth, we come to believe that God heals. It is only through this power that we can heal from all the hurts and pain of our past and present. Through this healing our sanity and serenity is restored and we realize the promises listed in Step Nine.

For today, I embrace the love, acceptance and healing of my Higher Power.

Strength in Equality

For our group purpose there is one ultimate authority – a loving God as God is expressed in our group conscience. Our leaders are but trusted servants; they do not govern. (FAA Tradition Two)

We may have been brought up in a family where our father's word was the final say. We may have felt that we were never heard.

When we come into FAA, we see that everyone is allowed to express his or her views, and we begin to develop trust. We begin to see God in others, and we experience God's loving presence. We learn that our voice matters too. We are accepted.

In every meeting, the leader is also a recovering food addict. The leader is not there to govern, but rather, to be of service to the group. This may also instill in us a sense of trust, because we know that the leader is not the ultimate authority. We can find our voice.

For today, I trust that God will be expressed in a loving way when an issue calls for a group conscience.

Finding My Higher Power

I struggled when I first came to FAA with the concept of a Higher Power. I knew about a power greater than myself because food was my higher power for too many years. It ruled my life. My experiences had proved this repeatedly.

I knew that there was some other power that ran this universe. It made the seasons change, the flowers bloom, the sun rise and set, and the planets rotate. This power had nothing to do with me. I tried to understand this power and got stuck.

I found that I did not need to understand this power. I didn't even have to believe in this power. All I had to do was make a decision to turn my will and my life over to a Power greater than myself. I don't have to make everything so complicated!

I have learned that God was always there for me, even when I didn't believe it. I quit giving my Higher Power my list of things I wanted. How presumptuous of me to think God needed me to tell him what was best for the world and me!

For today, I thank God for another day of abstinence and ask that I be shown God's will and given the power to carry that out.

Recognizing Balance

Recovery brings us balance. In early recovery we may not have felt this balance. We might have thought we were far too one-sided because we had to spend an inordinate amount of time planning, reporting, and preparing our food. When we gave up sugar, flour, and wheat, we had to jump feet first into the program. We trusted that the other parts of our lives would reap the benefits. We had to spend as much time thinking about and planning recovery as we used to spend thinking about food, which was all the time!

We planned and committed our food, prayed, read literature, and made phone calls. Love and service became our way of life. We studied the Twelve Steps. The more we kept doing the next right thing, the easier and less time consuming it became. Then one day we realized our life was indeed more balanced.

For today, I am grateful for my balanced life.

Until We Believe

Some of us come into the program with a strong spiritual base. Others enter these rooms with no prior connection to a Higher Power. If Step Two baffles us – "Came to believe that a Power greater than ourselves could restore us to sanity" – we can "act as if."

How do we practice "acting as if" in our daily lives? Even when we think that remaining abstinent is about willpower and not about finding a Higher Power, we can act as if we believe in something greater than ourselves. If food thoughts come, we can pray to our Higher Power to relieve our obsession, acting as if our prayers will be answered. If our weighed and measured meals leave us hungry or feeling deprived, we can act as if we have eaten just the right amount to feed our bodies with sound nutrition.

We are not restored to sanity immediately. Step Two gives us hope. Over time, we find that acting as if turns us into believing in something greater than our own egos.

For today, I "act as if" until I have a working relationship with a power greater than myself.

I Know What I Know

I don't know a lot. But one thing I know for sure is that I am powerless over addictive foods and my life is unmanageable when I am eating them. I am not powerless because of a lack of willpower, nor because I am a compulsive person (which I am), nor because of what I am feeling. I am powerless because my body has a certain biochemical reaction when I eat addictive foods.

When I eat these foods, my life becomes unmanageable. This is because my body does not want those things in there. It is difficult for me to manage my life when I am ingesting addictive substances. I make everything so complicated, when in fact it is simple. It is as simple as don't pick up no matter what and go to meetings.

For today, I accept the fact that I have a biochemical disease.

Our Biochemistry Is Not Unique

The desert sand rat obtains all of its nourishment from the leaves of the saltbush. Although this makes for a spartan diet, the sand rat, in his ability to adapt to his harsh environment, thrives. When raised in captivity, however, the sand rat overeats and develops health problems. The commercial food overwhelms the sand rat's sensitive biochemistry and triggers him to eat endlessly.

As a food addict, I also thrive on simple, unrefined foods. Refined foods, which others can handle, caused me to binge and ruin my health.

It was difficult to take Step One and admit I was powerless and acknowledge that I am so influenced by my biochemistry. I always blamed my emotions. But I noticed that there was (conveniently) always an emotion – happy or sad, bored or excited – that could set off my addiction.

Of course, because my disease progresses, I also need emotional and spiritual healing. But to experience full recovery, I must begin with the physical recovery that abstinence brings.

For today, I pray for continued abstinence that I may experience physical, emotional, and spiritual healing.

Becoming Acquainted With God

New to the program, I had belief in spirituality but no relationship with a personal Higher Power. The only image I had of a god was of a wise but stern old man in the sky who had more important matters at hand than my weight or food choices.

However, I was told that my Higher Power could be anything or anyone I wanted, as long as it was not my own ego. At first I tried to envision different manifestations of God: a bright light, an angel, the beauty of nature. While I could see the divine in these things, the image from my youth of God was ingrained in my psyche. I had to change my way of thinking and started to envision my Higher Power as warm and caring, like a loving parent or mentor.

I now turn my will and life over to God on a daily basis. God offers guidance, never condemnation. When I make unwise choices, God lets me learn the lessons of life but is always there to comfort, encourage, and reassure me.

Having a close, personal relationship with a loving God keeps me centered. I still experience the ups and downs of life, but I no longer careen out of control and into addictive self-destruction. I let God lead and, with trust, I follow.

For today, I give my will and my life over to God's loving care and guidance.

Let God Be in Control

Made a decision to turn our will and our lives over to the care of God as we understood God. (FAA Step Three)

When we take Step Three and give everything to God, an immediate shift in how we view ourselves and the world occurs. We can no longer live by the self-propulsion that had gotten us to the place of surrender. We had to stop. We had to quit playing God. We may have looked around and realized that we didn't know what our life meant anymore. What brought us joy now brings us sorrow. What we were once afraid of became the best thing for us. We begin to see the paradox of surrender and we begin to feel freedom.

We consciously let God be in charge. Some days the best prayer we can muster is, "God, I barely trust that you can handle this any better than I can, but I know that if I hold on to it, I will mess it up. So, I'm giving it to you." Other days, we trust fully that everything we need is already provided.

For today, I will be pleasantly surprised at how adept God is at running my life.

Just for Today

The past no longer needs to be a source of shame or guilt for us. No matter what mistakes we made or what opportunities we missed because of our addiction, they have brought us to where we are today. We cannot change nor forget what was, but we can use our experiences to learn. We can let go, forgive, and live a happy and joyous life today. The fellowship of FAA is a nurturing and safe haven for these healing processes and learning opportunities.

Our experiences can support rather than haunt us today. We can use them as learning tools for our recovery. The disease within us is rendered powerless as long as we are abstinent and working the program. We have no time for remorse. Today is a day in which we can forget all of the "should haves," "would haves," and "could haves." We are bright, alert, and eager for life's adventures.

For today, I thank God for the wisdom gleaned from past lessons and the gift of living joyously in the present.

Road to Achieving Manageability

"Abstinence can be an overwhelming prospect, and trying to absorb it can seem downright hopeless. A sponsor helps to share the load, and makes the task seem more manageable." (<u>Food Addicts Anonymous</u>, *Beginning the Journey*)

My modus operandi during years of attempting to recover from food addiction has been to go it alone. During my early days in FAA, I quickly discovered that the guidance I had been yearning for was in this fellowship. Here were people who knew how to manage their lives. They had years of experience in dealing with the object of their addiction on a daily basis. They knew how to plan, shop for, prepare, order, and eat the foods that support abstinence. They knew how to handle difficult situations that involved food. I finally accepted that I did not know how to do or be any of these things and that I needed their help desperately.

I have come to learn that I am my own worst sponsor. I made the decision to trust my sponsor, who had what I wanted and knew how to keep it. I learned to be teachable out of necessity, and I have stayed teachable because I see its results in others and myself.

For today, I am grateful for my sponsor and for this fellowship.

Remaining Centered

As I move forward in recovery, I become more emotionally centered. I still experience anxiety, but I don't freak out about freaking out.

I don't spiral up into space and then feel the need to bring myself down with food. I don't spiral down to the depths and then feel the need to bring myself up with food.

There is a tether to my center, and when I drift too far out, I follow the line back to serenity. I do this by remembering how much God loves me, listing all of the worthy things I've done so far in the day, making a gratitude list, and recalling the misery of addictive eating.

The longer I remain abstinent and in recovery, the easier this type of thinking becomes. I become more familiar with my emotional center and make it my reference point. When my center feels distant, I take action to gently draw myself back in. I remain in today, unafraid and trusting that I can be sane and free.

For today, I ask God to keep me aware of my emotions and to guide me back to my center when I stray too far.

Doing the Footwork

Footwork is like crossing a busy street. I can't just blindly cross in the middle of the street against heavy traffic and ask God to keep me from being hit. If I go to the intersection, obey the traffic light, look both ways, and then walk at a steady pace, I can reasonably expect that I can make it safely to the other side.

I need to trust the good judgment that God gave me. In order to take care of my food needs today, I have to take staying abstinent as seriously as staying safe on the street. Praying daily for guidance and willingness, I spend time planning, purchasing, preparing, and eating my meals.

After I have done the footwork, I can trust that God will continue to release me from the cravings for foods that are not in my best interest and get me safely through this day.

For today, I will do my part – the footwork, and let God do God's.

Reasoning No Longer Works

My food addiction does not listen to reason. I have been willing to suffer obesity, emaciation, stomach pains, deterioration of health, marital strife, and familial and social alienation, all for the sake of consuming my addictive foods.

I knew that the pleasure I attained from a binge was only a temporary illusion of escape from chronic physical, emotional, and spiritual pain. Bingeing did not give me real pleasure; it just numbed me out.

When the impulse to binge struck, all rational thought evaporated within seconds. A rush of excitement would electrify me. I would be transported to a world where time was suspended and consequences were irrelevant compared with the incomparable pleasure that I anticipated with that first bite. I was helpless. I was powerless.

But the pleasure of the first bite was indeed an illusion. And the excitement of anticipation quickly turned to humiliation and emotional paralysis.

Bingeing was not worth the price I paid over and over. I finally learned that reasoning is useless against the force of addiction. Resistance creates pain. Surrender alleviates it.

For today, I ask God to keep me aware of the hopeless battle of bingeing.

Trusting in a Higher Power

Weight loss was once my primary motivation for recovery. Vanity was my goddess. For a while, she served me well. Life's ups and downs were easier to take when I had the mirror's constant reassurance that I looked beautiful. Like all false gods, vanity eventually turned on me.

Before long, the novelty of being thin wore off. The mirror no longer inspired me, and I was cast adrift without a Higher Power. I could not stay abstinent. I ate, and I gained back the weight plus a little more. Before long, lost in a food fog, I forgot how vanity had betrayed me. I was excited about weight loss and once again bowed down before her.

Vanity served time after time to get me abstinent. However, she was never strong enough to keep me there. I finally learned: to stay in recovery, I need a God I can rely on, one who will stay by my side no matter what. I need a Higher Power who will love me absolutely and passionately no matter what I weigh or how I look and who will draw ever closer to me in times of trial.

For today, I pray to strengthen my connection with a Higher Power.

Filling the Spiritual Void

Addictive food was our false idol. It delivered a temporary illusion of serenity at a very high price. It claimed health, sanity, self-respect, and the chance to connect with others. It usurped the rightful place of a Higher Power who loves us without demanding sacrifice, a Higher Power who loves us for who we are, a Higher Power who supports us and rejoices in our well-being and happiness.

When we first become abstinent, we recognize the frightful depths of our spiritual abyss. The sense of loss and emptiness that some of us experience can be profound.

But we trust and remain calm. We allow that empty space to lie fallow, without rushing to fill it with activity or other diversion, and soon we find that it is filled with something far greater than what the food ever gave us.

For today, whenever I sense a spiritual void, I pray to open my heart to God.

The Power of Today

We remain abstinent one day at a time. That one day is not tomorrow, it is this 24-hour period. Despite tomorrow's promise of deliverance, tomorrow's abstinence has no power to help us. On the contrary, tomorrow's abstinence has perpetuated many a binge for many a food addict.

Lulled by the lie that I would start my abstinence tomorrow or in the very near future, my disease told me not to worry, eat freely, and have that last indulgence. The next day, I'd believe the same deceit. The belief that this was a temporary state kept me in the disease for a very long time.

In recovery, we learn to direct this power against our disease. This same power that kept us in bondage can now serve to keep us free. Although it is true that tomorrow's abstinence cannot help me, it is also true that tomorrow's binge cannot hurt me. Exactly as I remained in addiction just for today, I now abstain on a day at a time basis.

The food demon need not tempt nor torment me today. He is lulled by the belief that tomorrow he might be welcome again, but not today. To be free, today is all I need.

For today, I pray I choose freedom, not bondage.

New Friends for Life

One of the wonderful aspects of recovery from food addiction is waking up to the fact that the foods we once thought were our friends are really our enemies. No friend would let us maim ourselves, strip ourselves of our self-esteem, or isolate. No friend would rob us of our chance to live a fulfilling, prosperous, healthy life.

The foods we eat on the FAA food plan are wholesome and nourishing. We pray daily to distinguish our enemies from our friends. We pray daily for the strength to let go of the foods that sweetly call to us with the purpose of destroying us. As we stay abstinent with each passing day, we feel a renewed vitality that comes from properly feeding our body, mind, and spirit.

For today, I ask my Higher Power to protect me on this spiritual path of recovery.

A Daily Routine

Following the FAA food plan is basic to my recovery. Just as I wouldn't walk out of the house in the middle of a snowstorm without a coat, or in the middle of a heat wave with a coat, I wouldn't start my day without planning and preparing my food. Once my food has been committed to my sponsor, I am ready to open up the Food Addicts Anonymous Step Book. For today I will do more than just read the Step. I will commit to applying the Step to my daily living activities.

I now have the ability, courage, and clarity to be true to my word and to follow my heart. I know that my Higher Power will not put anything in my path that I am not ready to handle.

For today, I put down the reins of control and let my Higher Power lead me.

Powerlessness

Admitting powerlessness may feel humiliating, especially when we have felt we were in control!

The disease of food addiction is completely beyond our control. We are truly powerless over our addiction. If we refuse to acknowledge our powerlessness, we deprive ourselves of the one thing that will save us. And in doing so, we may lose everything. The disease may infect and destroy everything else. The only solution that we have found is to admit our powerlessness, become humble, and surrender to the process that will bring us a daily reprieve.

As we grow in recovery, we perceive the degree of powerlessness we have over events, people, the weather, our own thoughts and delusions, and the millions of other things beyond our control. It is humbling to accept that there is very little we have any command over. We can choose each day to focus on our recovery from our addictions by taking certain actions. We can learn to control our words, thereby changing our feelings and attitudes. We can choose to align our will with God's will for us.

For today, I know that I have power to change only my actions and my reactions.

Honesty

Living in denial is living dishonestly. When abuse and loss caused us pain, we often tried to bury them deeply in our memory. However, being untrue to ourselves in this way or dishonest emotionally allows the pain from the past to infect the present, causing bad choices and suffering. When we stuff our sorrow, grief, and anger, we deny ourselves the experiences of joy, happiness, and emotional freedom.

The only way out of this imprisonment is through it. Working the Steps with our sponsor is the way to safely go back and deal with the buried issues and frozen feelings. The Steps move us forward in our emotional development, allowing us to grow up.

Desiring the promises of the program encourages us to pursue freedom from the disease. We need to be honest, confront our guilt, and move toward forgiveness.

For today, I ask God to help me be emotionally honest.

Hearing the Message

As I start this day, I ask my Higher Power for the willingness to be abstinent. With abstinence, I have the ability to think clearly and follow my heart. I prepare what I need for the day to keep me from craving foods that are not in my best interest. If I do nothing else, I will stay abstinent no matter what. I trust that my Higher Power will handle all people, places, and situations that are beyond my control.

Today I will call my sponsor. I will go to a meeting, focus on positive people, and stay clear of negative people. Today I am grateful that I have chosen to hear the message of recovery of Food Addicts Anonymous.

Today I commit to being positive, kind, and compassionate. I am responsible for not only what goes into my mouth but also for what comes out of my mouth. I will not utter gossip nor put myself down. If I think negative thoughts, I will keep them in my head and refrain from saying them. If I have nothing nice to say to another person, I will be silent.

With abstinence from sugar, flour, and wheat and using the tools of the program, I can truly be an instrument of my Higher Power. The only way I can adopt an attitude of gratitude is to take the initiative and change.

For today, I will find the good in others and focus on the positive.

Believe in Miracles

"Expect a miracle" is how the saying goes, but a miracle was the last thing we expected when we were in our disease.

As we spend more time in recovery from food addiction, we begin to see the miracles in our lives. The blinders slowly fall away. We start to make daily gratitude lists of the little miracles that happen. When we come to a fork in the road that requires a decision, we can ask for a miracle and believe that it will appear.

Life is much sweeter when we can see the miracles in our lives. Recognizing miracles is a deeper, greater sweetness than we have ever experienced from sugar, flour or wheat.

For today, I am grateful for all of the miracles I can see in my life, thanks to my abstinence.

The Healthier Choice

There are only two ways to go: headed for the disease or away from it. There is no middle ground. There are no vacations or holidays. My disease wants me to think that there are easier, softer ways of working this program. The disease is patient. With all the cunning it has, it will wait on the sidelines for that one opening I give it, and without a second's pause it will step right in and whisk me back to the torment that I once knew all too well.

There may be days when I want to sit it out. I may want to rest for a spell and put the FAA program on hold for a while. I can't afford to do this. I can allow myself these feelings, but I need to find a way of moving past them. I can write about them and I can express them at meetings or with trusted friends. While I work through these feelings, I continue to work my program. I deserve nothing less.

By working the Twelve Steps, I can stay one step ahead of the disease.

For today, I remember I deserve abstinence.

Positive Changes

My first thoughts regarding changing my behavior were about letting go of the addictive food – getting abstinent. Following my food plan led to a change in me. The aggression, anger, depression, negativity, illness, irresponsibility, and laziness all seemed to leave me. I began to have consistency in my life.

I realized that I could change even more by doing a daily inventory and refraining from behaviors that I know are not God's will, such as gossiping, lying, and holding resentments. I cannot work this program selectively – I cannot choose the Steps I like and leave out the rest.

I am on a journey. I have a commitment to my Higher Power and to myself to work this program to the best of my ability. I need to be honest about my motives and behavior and make conscious efforts to engage in the process of change. I can't do it alone, and that's where the FAA fellowship comes in.

For today, I embrace all of the FAA program and trust I will be given a daily reprieve.

Complexity of Learning

The long form of the Third Tradition in Food Addicts Anonymous <u>The Steps to Recovery</u> states: "We are not a weight loss or weight gain program. We do not judge each other's abstinence or the shape of our bodies."

One of the difficulties we may have with abstinence is thinking that our fellow food addicts work a better program than we do. Sometimes we hear food addicts stress that what works for them will work for us. This is not necessarily so.

There is no one way to stay abstinent other than not picking up sugar, flour, and wheat. We strengthen our abstinence by going to meetings and talking to a sponsor. It may appear that some people who seemed to be working a great program have relapsed, whereas others appear to do very little and yet stay abstinent. But we all have to do a little of everything – go to as many meetings as possible, continue to do Step work, be of service, and sponsor others.

We learn not to compare our abstinence to that of others.

For today, I refrain from comparing myself to other food addicts.

A Momentous Decision

Made a decision to turn our will and our lives over to the care of God as we understood God. (FAA Step Three)

Step One gave us the freedom of our powerlessness over our food addiction. Step Two assured us a Power greater than ourselves could restore us to sanity. Now in the Third Step, we can take a positive move forward. This Step is not complicated. I struggled for years trying to figure out how to turn my will and life over. Many times I would take back the very problems I had turned over, thinking I could do a better job than my Higher Power. Turning over our will is turning our *thinking* and our *actions* over.

This decision is the cornerstone of individual recovery. How can we make such an important decision when we haven't even been able to decide whether to have green beans or broccoli for dinner? The answer is we have tried everything else, and nothing has brought us long term abstinence. When we are convinced this is all that is left for us to do, we will make the decision.

For today, I thank my Higher Power that this spiritual program heals me on a daily basis.

It Was More Than Exercise

Before FAA, we may have tried to compensate for our bingeing by over exercising. Perhaps we became obsessed with working out. If for some reason we could not work out on a particular day, that day was ruined, and fear of weight gain would consume us. We may have attempted to restrict our food intake to compensate for not exercising that day.

We were driven by the treadmill. We may have turned down invitations to do other things because we had to be at the gym. What a horrible way to live. If we weren't thinking about food, we were figuring out how to work it off through exercise. We had no control over our food, and since we were so fearful of weight gain, we thought that maybe we could control the consequences of overeating by purging through exercise.

At FAA we learn that because we weigh and measure our food, we do not need to weigh and measure our bodies. Today by eating a plan of sound nutrition and applying the Steps to our lives, we no longer have to abuse our bodies with excess exercise.

For today, I celebrate the life recovery has given me.

Looking for Different Results

"Diets became our Higher Power, only to fail us again and again." (<u>Food Addicts Anonymous</u>, *Who is a Food Addict?*)

What a sad plight it is to worship a false god – sugar, flour, and wheat. In doing so, our disease has led us to deprive ourselves of nutrition or to believe that everything would be OK if we ate. The false promises made by our disease repeatedly drove us to the desperation of bingeing and weight gain.

Time and time again, we believed the voice of our disease and were devotees. We relentlessly pursued diets, always expecting different results. Even mid-binge, we often considered ourselves still to be on a diet!

Obsession with food and weight enslaved us. We blamed ourselves for our endless failures. We wanted to be loved, and we believed we could earn the love of others by controlling our food and weight.

Our Higher Power has always been with us, but the voice of the disease drowned out the voice within. When we started listening to that voice, the voice of our true self, we were led to recovery. The only thing we gave up in recovery was hopelessness. And we gained a healthy body weight and the daily blessing of nourishing, satisfying, abstinent meals.

For today, I thank my loving Higher Power for revealing the tyranny of diets.

From Rags to Riches

When we first become abstinent, we may feel impoverished – we no longer use the substances that were our "everything." We may feel bereft, alone, and frightened. We may fear that our needs will never be met.

In truth, we were so focused on food that we never experienced the riches of life. The sugar, flour, and wheat provided false security. Even when we thought that our binge foods were making us feel good, they eventually brought us to despair. We didn't notice the true riches in our lives. No matter how many times we tried to deal with our obsession, we never got anywhere. In fact, we often ended up in a prison of self-loathing, isolation, and desperation.

When we are free of our feelings of shame and worthlessness, we come to believe that our Higher Power wants our lives to be rich in every way. We can see that we experience an abundant life, overflowing with everything that is good: a clear mind, serenity, wonderful relationships, fulfilling work, beauty, and freedom – in short, our heart's desire. We have only to be open and willing to receive these gifts.

For today, I trade my rags of addiction for the richness of recovery.

Looking For the Easier, Softer Way

What freedom Tradition Three gives the food addict. There are no prepackaged foods, no dues to pay, no before-and-after pictures. We are equal and bound together by our common addiction to sugar, flour, and wheat.

We may have spent inordinate amounts of money on weight-loss programs. Many of us were lifetime members of various weight-loss clubs, or we may have purchased hundreds of diet books. We may have spent money on pills as well, hoping that they would control our appetites, as advertised. Instead, such pills usually kept us up at night, giving us more hours to binge!

The Twelve Steps of FAA allow us to heal from the ravages of our food addiction. The program is a spiritual way of life. Practicing this Tradition Three brings us personal recovery.

For today, I thank my Higher Power for my desire to stop eating addictive foods one day at a time.

Our Concept of God

In FAA, we get to choose the God of our understanding. We may feel God in the love and serenity we hear at our FAA group meeting. Or we may feel God as an infinite force who created the universe. Or we may not be able to define God but nevertheless can turn our will over to him.

Some of us come into recovery with a fairly well developed concept of God. But our faith did not keep us abstinent. We needed to start over. Perhaps we needed to start with the idea that a Power greater than ourselves existed. That is all that is asked of us and that is all it took to make a beginning. With just that much, we can begin to work the Steps.

By the grace of our Higher Power, we continue to stay abstinent and active in the rooms of FAA. We live the Steps in our daily lives. We are grateful to have found a solution that isn't just another diet.

For today, I ask God to help me remember that I came to FAA spiritually bankrupt and that spiritual food is necessary for my journey.

Progressing Through the Steps

We may not have a very good track record when it comes to making decisions. Most of us have spent years turning our will and our life over to addictive foods. We thought if we stuffed our feelings, we could avoid the harsh realities of life. The consequences didn't deter us – weight gain, failed relationships, lost dreams. We just kept on eating.

In Step One, we face the powerlessness and unmanageability of our disease.

In Step Two, we accept that our behavior was insane. We need to be restored to sanity by a power greater than ourselves. That power was not sugar, flour, or wheat.

In Step Three, we make a decision to turn our thoughts and actions over to God, as we understand God. We may have no conception of God. Our sponsors may suggest that we write a description of how we understand God and what we want from God.

For today, I may not understand God, but God understands me. I am abstinent, grateful, serene, and loved.

Glimmers of Gratitude

Before I even got out of bed this morning, I was thinking about uncomfortable situations. With each thought, fear and anxiety mounted inside me. I started thinking of going outside or going somewhere, going anywhere. My mind was racing.

Even with my head going crazy, I planned my food for the day. Then, I meditated and prayed. Soon I found myself taking a small action. I started to write a gratitude list. I wrote down all the beautiful, enjoyable people and places I could think of. I wrote down my good health, including how my body no longer ached from bingeing the night before. I began to hear the birds singing in my yard. My fears and racing thoughts lessened. As the list grew, so did my inner peace. Serenity was filling me.

As a recovering food addict, I strive to live one day at a time and look for the small things in life that really make me happy. This is not a theory. This is a solution. What a gift to no longer be searching for the answers.

For today, I make a gratitude list, beginning with my gratitude for the help my Higher Power gives me to abstain, which gives me my life and good health.

Desire Unlocks the Door

The only requirement for FAA membership is a desire to stop eating addictive foods. (FAA Tradition Three)

Tradition Three tells us that anyone who wishes to be free of food addiction is welcome at FAA meetings. We are not an exclusive club – we are an inclusive fellowship. Our doors are open to anyone who wants to benefit from the shared experience of other food addicts, regardless of sex, religion, political ideology, or social standing.

This singleness of purpose is what keeps the fellowship of Food Addicts Anonymous strong. We do not weaken our fellowship by judging each other's abstinence or appearance. We will not be divided through enlistment in other causes, and Tradition Three guides us in this resolve.

FAA has stayed strong through the devotion of its members to upholding the Twelve Steps and Twelve Traditions. We know how important it is to stay together and to continue to hold meetings, so that our brothers and sisters who are mired in active food addiction can find relief. We have a solution for the problem of food addiction.

For today, I uphold Tradition Three by remembering that our primary purpose is to help other food addicts.

As Simple as One, Two, Three

A wonderful recovery idea is to be nice to ourselves. The habit of being hard on one's self is a difficult one to break, but we can learn to break this habit through practicing the Twelve Steps.

When we feel ourselves losing our perspective, we can get back on track by being our own best friend – that is, by treating ourselves with the love and attention that we would show to a treasured friend.

The most precious gift we can give ourselves today is staying abstinent.

When we are trying to let go and let God, we can remember this simplified version of the first three Steps:

- I can't
- God can
- I think I'll let God

For today, I am kind and gentle with myself and show gratitude for my new FAA life.

Trusting the Process

There will be moments when I will stumble. There will be moments when I will fall. There will be moments when I will doubt my progress. I need to remember that I am human and that this self-doubt and imperfection is part of my makeup. It also reinforces my need to stick close to others in Food Addicts Anonymous and to work this program of recovery to the best of my ability. I can't do it alone.

In those times when I do stumble and fall, it is the perfect occasion to reflect on my growth so far. Can I see the change in myself? Can I see how far I've come? More often than not I need to rely on the clearer vision of those who have walked the path before me. They can offer me the gentle reinforcement I need so much in those slippery moments.

I need to continue putting one foot in front of the other. I need to work the Twelve Steps. I need to continue weighing and measuring my food. Most important of all, I need to trust the process. My Higher Power has not brought me this far to leave me flat.

For today, I trust the process, knowing that if I put the effort into working my program, I thrive.

Set the Stage

To avoid relapse, I have learned to set the stage.

I was told long ago to act as if I were happy being a food addict in recovery and to do so until I actually believed it. I rolled my eyes, thinking that it would never happen for me, but I was desperate and willing to take suggestions.

I felt like a liar for acting as if. But then I started to look back over my life and recalled the many, many times I had "acted as if"…not as if I were in recovery, but, rather, as if I were a "normal" eater. How many times had I gone through a drive-through "acting as if" I was ordering for a family of four? How many times have I "acted as if" everything was fine when I was really dying inside? The truth is that I am very experienced at "acting as if." So, in recovery, I can "act as if" in order to stay sane and reap the promises I so deserve.

For today, I act as if my life depends on my abstinence, because it does.

Fourth Step Inventory

Made a searching and fearless moral inventory of ourselves. (FAA Step Four)

We may have spent a lot of time getting ready for Step Four getting lost in the maze of possible approaches. Should we answer the questions in our Step book? Should we write our life history? Should we write a list of people we resent?

We may become paralyzed by the number of choices thinking that we must do it perfectly. Somehow, the task becomes so important that we never actually find enough time to do it!

Our sponsors may urge us to keep things simple. They encourage us to pray and listen when beginning our Step Four. We come to accept the fact that our writing will not be perfect. But we can begin anyway. We may find that once we write the first sentence, the thoughts flow.

What we share from Step Four with our sponsor helps us take Step Five. We then find ourselves moving on to the subsequent Steps. Taking the Twelve Steps places us on the road to recovery. We no longer need to escape our uncomfortable emotions with addictive behaviors.

For today, I ask God to grant me the courage to take baby steps.

The Momentum of Recovery

Often we hear at meetings, "It is easier to stay abstinent than to get abstinent." The law of conservation of momentum applies to addiction as well as to the material realm. Once we are rolling in abstinence, if we keep doing what we are doing, one day at a time, we will keep coasting along. We may not always be coasting, though; there will be rough spots and hills to ascend. But the momentum of recovery does much to carry us at these times.

The corollary, of course, is that a body in the food tends to remain in the food. The momentum of an isolated system upon which no external forces act does not change. Here is the key to escape. The program teaches us to break the isolation. To reach out to fellow food addicts. To open our minds and let new ideas enter. To open our hearts and let hope enter. To reach out to our Higher Power and let our Higher Power redirect us.

The laws of the universe work both to create and destroy. In recovery, we allow the fundamental forces of the universe to sustain us rather than defeat us. If we are abstinent, we allow positive momentum to keep us on that blessed path.

For today, I thank God for keeping me on the abstinent path.

Emotional Honesty

Living in denial is living a lie. Pain from past abuses and losses is often buried deep within our psyche. Pain infects the present, leading to bad choices and suffering. Repressing the bad feelings also buries the good feelings. We may deny the sorrow, grief, and anger, but we also deny ourselves the happiness and emotional freedom we could experience.

If we have become proficient at repression, developing emotional honesty is especially challenging. We have used our addiction to distract us from the unhealed pain within, but in reality we were controlled by it, subjected to its tendency to surface in explosive outbursts.

The only way out is through. We need to be honest about our past losses and hurts, express our feelings, look at our part, and move toward forgiveness and release. By sharing our Fourth Step inventory with our sponsor, we can safely go back into our past and deal with our buried issues and frozen feelings.

The actions that we take when we work the Steps move us forward emotionally. In effect, we grow up. This work is well worth the effort; emotional honesty sets us free to experience joy.

For today, I ask God for the courage to seek emotional honesty in my recovery.

My Constant Companion

I need to take FAA and my Higher Power everywhere I go, lest I start believing the voice of my disease. My Higher Power always wants to raise me up, whereas my disease always wants to hold me down.

One minute my disease tells me that I am svelte, like a ballet dancer. The next minute it tells me that I am hideous and should hide in a corner. The disease causes constant commotion in my head. Without abstinence, I am more vulnerable to the voice of disease, which urges me to take that first bite of candy or cake or French bread. My disease is a liar and never wants what is best for me.

On my own, I am defenseless against my disease. But with God at my side I am safe. Any time, anywhere, I can ask my Higher Power to lift my diseased thoughts. My Higher Power is always there to help me. All I have to do is ask.

For today, I take my Higher Power with me everywhere I go.

Freedom

What does it mean to me when I say "freedom from the bondage of self?"

I am free to enjoy the life that I have been given today. I am free to notice the beauty that surrounds me, the kindness of others, and the grace of a soaring bird. I am free to be the best person that I can be. I can watch my strengths and assets grow as I practice the Steps in all of my affairs.

I am free of the bondage of my character defects as I turn them over to my Higher Power, one day at a time. And I can make amends when I need to do that.

I am free to live my life in tune with nature, the universe, and the God of my understanding.

I am free from the obsession about food, calories, diets, bingeing, and purging. I am free from the guilt and shame of addictive and compulsive eating.

For today, I include abstinence and turning my life over to God in my recipe for freedom.

At Peace Today

Today I have peace in my heart because I accept that I am a food addict.

I no longer need to constantly think of controlling what, when, where, and how much I will eat. I am no longer a slave to my binge foods. I have more choices today than to eat as a response to my life.

What freedom acceptance has given me. The fight is over. To know that I am an addict is like a beam of light in the darkness that enveloped me most of my life. The light of hope shines brightly within me today.

Today I do not have to spend time desperately trying to find something, anything, to take away the craziness brought about by my obsession with food.

Accepting that I am a food addict is saving my life. I am blessed with the freedom of choice today. I have finally found a workable solution that enables me to make healthy choices – both about food and about my life.

For today, I am grateful for the peace that comes with knowing there is a solution.

Remember to Pause

Abstinence gives me clarity of mind that was unknown to me when I was bingeing. Everything is more vivid: what I see, what I taste, what I smell, and, especially, what I feel. Before abstinence, I found that any strong emotion would send me to the food. The gift of this program is that it gives me pause between the feeling and the binge.

With abstinence, I can ask myself, "What is this uncomfortable feeling?" I can contact my sponsor, call another recovering addict, write about what I am feeling, work a Step, and pray. I pray to accept all of my feelings as normal and human. I can now experience any feeling and know that with my Higher Power's help, it will pass and I will grow from the experience.

For today, I live one day at a time through the grace of my Higher Power.

Channeling Our Anger

Anger is a human emotion. It can tell us that there is something going on that needs our attention. Anger is not a character defect, but the way in which we express it can be.

At times, we may use anger as a way to gain power. Or we respond in anger when instead we are really grieving, sad, or fearful. We may be angry at a vulnerability that we see in a loved one or in ourselves.

We have learned that anger has no power to control our food addiction. There is only one power that can combat food addiction – our Higher Power.

When we are angry, we can turn it over to our Higher Power and get out of the way. Then we can know peace. Anger is useful if it draws our attention to something we can control, but it is not useful for those things that we are powerless over, like our food addiction.

For today, I choose to open the door to a happy useful life free of misdirected anger and resentment.

Neither On nor Off a Diet

Today, thanks to FAA, I am neither on nor off a diet. I am not restricting my food to compensate for past bingeing, nor bingeing in reaction to past restrictions.

Today I neither gorge on my addictive foods nor attempt to subsist entirely on low calorie or highly processed diet foods. I am neither counting nor discounting calories.

I exercise today for the joy of movement and for maintaining health, not to burn calories or lose weight.

I neither starve nor graze endlessly today. I am not famished or drugged with excess food. Today I nourish my body with regular, satisfying, abstinent meals.

I am respectful towards my body and strive for balance in my life. The results are that I am living a life of moderation, peace, and stability.

For today, I nurture my body and strive for balance.

Floating on a Pink Cloud

When we are newcomers to abstinence, we may experience a type of euphoria that some FAA members refer to as a *pink cloud*. We can liken that phrase, *pink cloud*, to the puffy pink cherry blossoms that bloom in the spring. We know that these trees bloom for only a short time, but we can remember them throughout the year. So too, we can remember the spring of our abstinence by staying abstinent. We can see and appreciate the beauty that surrounds us.

Every day of abstinence is a day in which we can experience peace and serenity. We may have to face some unhappy events in our lives, but we have an inner core that remains happy and free no matter what happens. We begin to believe that the world is a beautiful place, and every day we can find something that brings us joy.

The cherry blossoms are fleeting, but we can experience their beauty, just as we can experience that pink-cloud feeling, if we remain open, honest, and abstinent.

For today, I embrace my happy, joyful, and peaceful thoughts.

Establishing Boundaries

In addiction, we lacked clear personal boundaries, failing to recognize where we stop and where others begin. We used food to compensate, to keep others away or to avoid obligations, often when a simple no would have sufficed.

In recovery, we learn to establish healthy boundaries. We learn to define our obligations and commitments to others. We become comfortable asserting our bottom line. Personal integrity increases as we honor both the commitments we accept and our right to refuse. We come to trust in relationships, to have faith in the give and take of healthy interactions.

Once we have established healthy boundaries, we must remain humble and honest in order to maintain them. We learn to respect others' boundaries as well as our own. At the end of each day, as part of our daily Tenth Step inventory, we can consider whether we protected ourselves from overcommitment and whether we honored the commitments that we made.

For today, I ask for help to maintain the serenity that comes from respecting my boundaries and honoring commitments.

Cravings vs. Obsession

In recovery, we learn to distinguish a physical craving from an emotional obsession.

During detoxification, we are likely to experience physical cravings because addictive substances were in our body. Once we have gone through detoxification, physical cravings may arise if too many hours elapse between meals.

An emotional obsession, in contrast, is a deeply ingrained reaction to the stresses of life. Fortunately, it is not as compelling as a physical craving. If food calls to us and there is no physical basis, then we can ask ourselves whether we are anxious, depressed, angry, lonely, or tired. Once we identify the feeling, we can take action to change the feeling or to turn it over to our Higher Power. We learn to walk through discomfort. As we develop these new coping skills, we are blessed with emotional stability, and the emotional obsession fades.

Turning to addictive food is never the answer as it feeds the fire of both, and then we must again face the challenge and discomfort of detoxification. With practice, we become more centered, until living an obsession-free life is second nature.

For today, I ask my Higher Power to help me to recognize my feelings, and to respond constructively.

Choosing to Live Life

I choose to spend more time each day in prayer and meditation so that each moment I live and each action I take reflects my Higher Power. I have never had this freedom before. My addiction had command of my life and made the choices for me.

I choose to make conscious contact with my Higher Power an ongoing part of my life. Only in this way will I be able to find my true place in the world. I choose to shed self-centeredness, fear, negativity, compulsivity, and any other character defect that stands in the way of conscious contact with my Higher Power. The Twelve Step path shows me how to do this and makes it possible for me to a have a choice in my life today.

Today I choose to continue my commitment to the Twelve Step way of life, one day at a time. Today I choose to live with an open heart in harmony with my Higher Power. Today I choose to pass this peace on to others through positive action, compassion, and acceptance. In this way, I will be able to keep the gift that my Higher Power and other recovering food addicts have so freely given me.

Today I am choosing to carry out whatever my Higher Power asks of me.

For today, I choose to live a happy, joyous, and free life as the willing partner of my Higher Power.

Celebrating Our Differences

When I first came into FAA, I was a snob. I was narrow-minded and intolerant of people who were different. I did not necessarily see myself as better than, but I saw others as less than. I heard people share about their Higher Power. I thought, "How could anyone believe that way?" I was judgmental and intolerant.

While I focused on being judgmental, I was unable or unwilling to look at myself.

Before long, however, I really listened and watched. I lowered my defenses, and many of those people I judged became my best friends.

Having low self-esteem caused me to shrink from interaction with people who I felt were highly intelligent. The more I stay around and work on recovery, the more I respect my intelligence and myself. The highly intelligent people I meet today no longer intimidate me. In fact, I have friends from all walks of life. We are equal in wanting to work this program and to live the abstinent life – happy and free.

Each of us has a unique story. Some people tell stories I can easily relate to, and others tell stories that I can only imagine. From each one I learn. We teach each other.

For today, I stay abstinent, keep an open mind, and celebrate our differences.

Caring for Ourselves

As children, we depended on others for protection, love, and nourishment. Some of us received plenty; many received less. In the end, we all survived.

Today we are adults, but we have not lost our need for love and caring. Today we are not dependent on our parents or on anyone else to give us what we need. Today we are responsible for taking care of ourselves.

The most important way in which we take care of ourselves is by eating abstinently. When we eat addictively, we are not respecting ourselves. Then we rationalize that we are too overwhelmed, too ill, too distracted, too sad, or too lost to be nurturing.

The moment we say no to addictive foods, we are being true to ourselves. We are embracing who we are. Within us, a deep and powerful love unfolds. We experience self-love. We are no longer alone. We have a reason to live. We have a reason to stay in recovery, one day at a time. We have ourselves.

For today, I care for my precious self, a beloved child of God.

Leap of Faith

When I realize that I am overwhelmed because I am living in an obsession of the day, I write down my thoughts and place them in my God box. It helps me to practice letting go and letting God. I put my God box away as an act of faith that God cares about every aspect of my life.

If I continue to entertain thoughts about whatever is not going my way, I remember that it is no longer my job to try to figure out what to do. God is working on it, and when the time is right, I'll get my answer.

My life is in God's hands. God knows better than I do, so I will let God handle all my problems today.

For today I find peace in recognizing that acceptance is the answer to all my problems.

Commitment

Commitment is something we tried to avoid before coming into FAA. We soon learn, however, that in committing to FAA and to the food plan, we may be able to achieve what we want out of life. It opens us up to going beyond our comfort zone.

Commitment means going to meetings even when we are feeling tired or lazy; giving service when we think we do not have enough time in the day; and avoiding that first bite of food not on the food plan, even when our disease tells us it's okay.

Commitment is doing what we say we will do, even if the outcome is not exactly how we planned it. More importantly, we accept the outcome and look for the lesson we need to learn.

Today, when we make a commitment to others and to ourselves it is always a win-win situation. We can love and feel loved. Life is not always easy, but as long as we are committed to the FAA way and to abstinence, we can work through any problem.

For today, I honor my commitment to FAA, abstinence, and myself.

We Are Not Afraid

We recognize and focus on our strengths. We don't hold back on following our intuition. We rise above our defenses. We crawl out from beneath the darkness of our fears and into the light. We share what we have been so freely given.

We are not afraid to take risks, to embrace life, to love each other. If we do not take the risk of being hurt, then we will not have the opportunity to experience the joy of love and intimacy. Being vulnerable builds our character.

A more textured life can open up for us. We are no longer afraid of who we are. We are free to explore our interests and to acknowledge our desires. We are willing to try those things that seem right for us.

For today, I trust that my Higher Power is in charge and knows what is best for me.

Trusting My Higher Power

I trust in my Higher Power and work to develop a stronger connection with that presence. I trust my Higher Power is good and wants what is best for me. I invite the presence of my Higher Power into my very core.

Where do I find my Higher Power? How does my Higher Power manifest? By listening. By being quiet. By taking time to just be by myself. In this place, I let the cares of the day drift away. I listen to that soft voice, and the more that I heed that voice, the stronger the voice becomes. I allow my Higher Power to rest with me.

With time, everything changes – even me. I let go and trust in my Higher Power, because my Higher Power is the only constant in my life.

For today, I develop a stronger connection with my Higher Power by being still.

Taking Inventory

Writing our Step Four inventory allows us to examine our lives.

In writing our inventory, we may realize that we have actually become comfortable with being uncomfortable. At least being uncomfortable is predictable. In fact, we may have grown to actually like some of our defects of character.

We may also find while writing our inventory that we have been harboring a lot of fear. Fear of being abandoned, fear of being yelled at, fear of being poor, fear of being rejected, and fear of not being loved.

We can walk through our mental blind spots and our fears with our sponsor holding one hand and our Higher Power holding the other. God helps us make changes when we become willing to change.

Every day we can strive for further emotional and spiritual growth that will allow God to help us grow up. Step Four is a powerful tool of recovery.

For today, I thank God for the gift of this life-changing Step work in FAA.

The Breath of Life

Food can be pleasurable, and it effectively satisfies physical hunger. However, as a food addict, I attempted to meet all of my needs – physical, emotional, and spiritual – through food.

I ate when I needed sleep or rest. I drank something sweet when I was thirsty. I ate warm foods when I was cold and cold foods when I was warm. I even turned to food when I simply needed to take a deep breath or two.

I had difficulty moving through the day. Getting up in the morning, leaving for work, arriving at work, returning home, starting any new task or activity – all of these transitions evoked anxiety and the desire to eat. It allowed for little breathing space. Eating was my default option whenever I was faced with indecision.

Admitting I am powerless over my food addiction and living in recovery has changed me. Today I use new and very different ways to meet the next challenge.

Taking a deep breath, or several, is so much more effective than bingeing. Now when I need a little breather, I do not eat – I breathe! Breath is life, and I am truly living.

For today, I ask God to remind me to breathe as I remain abstinent and move through my day.

Embracing the Process

Fear has sometimes stopped my growth in recovery. Sometimes fear freezes me. I become fear-filled and unable to move forward if I look at an issue with a negative eye. When I approach Step Four, the not knowing what is going to happen, or worse yet, knowing I will have to honestly look at the choices I have made and relive them blocks my progress. Instead of dreading the process, I need to look forward to bringing out what I fear most in order to put it in my past and learn from it.

I've heard a fellow FAA member say, "Within me there is my darkness and my light. I want to list both of these, give thanks for my light, and then offer my darkness to God to be removed and replaced with more of God's light." If I am truly honest, my light will be much stronger than my darkness. If I am patient and thorough, this Step will cleanse me and allow me to move on to living a life of peace and serenity.

For today, I look at my strengths that come from knowing who I am as a result of applying the Steps to my life.

Resisting Relapse

When I am faced with uncomfortable feelings, relapse looms on the horizon. Rather than press through the scary feelings, rather than set aside my pride and ask for help, I resist forward motion by pulling into myself again and reverting to old behaviors. I begin to isolate, forgetting that I am not alone.

What terrible thing do I not want to face? Why won't I pick up a pencil and write it on paper, getting it out of my heart and off my mind? Is it possible that my thinking can be twisted, that I am being held prisoner by something that is not true or something that is simply in my head?

How strong is this Power greater than myself? Stronger than the fear that I allow to paralyze me? When I recognize fear, what prevents me from asking God to remove it from me? What prevents me from trusting God, others, and myself?

Why can't I be honest enough to say, "I'm having some trouble here" and humble enough to say, "Please help me?"

Relapse brings up these questions for me.

The next question is what choices will I make today? Will I hold onto my will, or will I surrender my will and my life over to the care of God?

For today, I say a two-word prayer — God, help.

Respecting Group Autonomy

Each group should be autonomous except in matters affecting other groups or FAA as a whole. (FAA Tradition Four)

Tradition Four applies the fundamental principle of FAA that every group is equal to every other group. No one group dictates. Each has an equal voice.

The group makes decisions and resolves any conflicts independently through open discussion to reach a group conscience, with each member participating equally. Since the groups are the building blocks of the FAA structure, the action of each group is vital to the fellowship.

There is one exception and restriction to the group's total freedom of action. It will always act in the best interest of the fellowship and do nothing that could destroy FAA's unity of purpose. The group will not deny entrance to any member, affiliate with or promote other causes, accept outside contributions, become professional in Twelfth Step work, or violate anonymity.

For today, I honor the principles set forth in Tradition Four.

Seeing the Gifts in Others

People are multifaceted. We are only able to see a small part of who people really are. We never know what has helped to form another human being – the hurts, the mistreatment, the ailments, the disappointments.

Each person brings something different into our lives. Each person teaches us in some way, even if we don't think that we like the lesson. We strive to be open to the unique gifts that each person brings. We strive to be open to different cultures, ideas, lifestyles, and levels of recovery.

Just as we don't want others judging us, we refrain from judging others. We remember that we are all imperfect human beings who are doing our very best with what we know. We walk gently and keep our minds open to the gifts offered by each person with whom we come in contact. We can learn to accept the fragility in others and in ourselves.

For today, I focus on recovery without judgment of others or myself.

Staying in Recovery

Sometimes I hear people share at meetings about eating food that is "abstinent" or "non-abstinent." But in reality, food cannot be either. It is just food. We, on the other hand, can be abstinent or non-abstinent.

Today I gladly remain abstinent. I abstain from those substances that I find myself craving, namely sugar, flour, and wheat, because I am addicted to them. However, sometimes my disease tries to get to me through the back door by telling me that since a particular binge food does not contain sugar, flour, or wheat, then it's okay. But why would I eat those things? Where would it lead? It would lead to cravings either by making me hungrier for more or for something else.

I abstain from behaviors that might cause me cravings, such as overeating, volume eating, undereating, and spacing my meals too far apart. Using the FAA food plan, weighing and measuring my food, and following instructions make it possible for me to abstain from these behaviors.

FAA is teaching me that I am responsible for my own recovery. I am not a victim. I suffer from this disease only if I choose to. I am not powerless over my choices, nor am I powerless over my behavior. I am powerless over being a food addict.

For today, I am grateful for the freedom of having choices.

I Am Not My Disease

An important part of my recovery from food addiction has been learning how to identify my disease. I have learned that anything that makes me feel bad about myself is my disease. Before abstinence, I would chalk up the negativity to circumstances, how I was raised, my sensitive nature, you name it. Now, I am starting to see that I am not my disease. God is healing me, and in the process, I'm seeing glimpses of my true self.

When I become aware of my disease talking to me, I immediately turn it over to my Higher Power's care. Then I return to the present moment. The disease cannot live in the present, only the past, or the future. When I try to fight my disease or reason with it, I get sucked in and start to believe what it says to me.

Now I know that I can talk to my sponsor about what the disease is saying to me. In the safety of that relationship, I always see how crazy and irrational my disease is. It's fascinating to see the difference when I expose the disease to the light. What seemed believable in my head becomes ridiculous and loses all its power when spoken out loud to my sponsor.

For today, I turn my negative thoughts over to my Higher Power and live in the present.

Warriors, Not Worriers

We were filled with fear. We were worriers. Eating masked the fear but deepened the darkness. Our fears are revealed in early abstinence.

In our Fourth Step inventory, we expose fear to the light of reason. Courageously releasing the fear of fear, we can examine our issues. We then discover that most of our fears are only shadows.

We see that real threats are best faced directly. We realize that we are more protected and secure by facing our fears than by fleeing from them. We come to see that the greatest danger to our well-being, which we were once so helpless against or oblivious to, is living in active addiction.

In abstinence, we are not protected from all dangers. Life involves risks. But we no longer live in fear. We come out from the shadows. We take what rational action we can to protect ourselves from real threats. And we trust that God will guide us when life inevitably does present a fearful challenge.

We do not need strength to overcome fear. We need only courage, which comes from trusting the process of working the Steps and from faith in our Higher Power's love and protection. To worry is to let go of God's hand.

For today, I ask God to make me a warrior instead of a worrier.

One Day at a Time

I can do this today. My Higher Power has shown me that I can. I can pray for abstinence and guidance. I can experience freedom from the pain of addiction.

Today I can prepare and eat three healthy meals and a metabolic and spend the rest of the time living my life. I can cope with the emotions that come up when I stop stuffing them down. I can reach out to another food addict, go to a meeting, call a sponsor, or read recovery literature.

Today I do not have to control the world and the people around me. I know that I am responsible only for my actions and myself.

Today I will focus on the present and live in the solution. If I think too much about the future, and never eating sugar again as long as I live, I set myself up. I am moving away from recovery and into diet mentality. If I dwell on the past with its failures, I am surrounding myself with negativity.

For today, I am grateful for turning my life and my will over to the care of my Higher Power.

Learning Lessons

Abstinence gives me the clarity I need to move through today. The food fog has lifted. My Higher Power can work through me. I am equipped to deal with life, come what may.

If I venture down a path that is not in my best interest, I will perceive this in time so that I can change my direction. I no longer stumble along, oblivious until circumstances grow dire. With the gift of abstinence, I can read the signs and go with the flow. I learn from life's lessons. There are no mistakes.

For today, I thank God for the lessons sent and for the ability through abstinence to be an apt student.

Taking the Fifth

Admitted to God, to ourselves, and to another human being the exact nature of our wrongs. (FAA Step Five)

So many times I know what I need to do but do not do it. Our literature states that "the exact nature of our wrongs and what motivates us to continue repeating the same behavior over and over again, hoping things will magically change are what sabotage us." We sometimes need help in knowing what to do next. We learn to share our secrets, because they feed our disease. Instead, by sharing, we have a chance to heal.

For many of us, a Fifth Step is the beginning of learning how to be honest with someone else. Replacing denial with honesty is not easy but with the foundation of abstinence and the first four Steps, we are capable. We can begin to be honest when we admit our powerlessness.

This process of sharing our inventory helps us become willing to change not only our food but also our attitudes, actions, personality traits, and character traits. Talking frankly with another person requires humility, trust, and honesty, all of which are keys to our spiritual growth.

For today, I take Step Five and continue to grow and recover from food addiction.

If You Want What We Have

When we strive to get abstinent and grow spiritually, we seek out a sponsor who has what we want. We look at his or her recovery program and ask for guidance in helping us stay abstinent and in working the Steps. But just how open-minded are we to suggestions?

Recovery from food addiction and daily growth require that we let go of what we think is right for us and open our minds to what our sponsor suggests. This is not always easy. Our sponsor reminds us, "If you want what I have, do what I do." When we hear this we may be thinking, "But I'm different."

Eventually, we throw up our hands in frustration when we can't achieve the joy in abstinence that we see our sponsor achieving. Finally, we surrender – totally surrender – to our sponsor's suggestions. We weigh, measure, and report our food daily. We utilize the tools of recovery. Ultimately, we find the joy and freedom from food addiction that we have so desperately been seeking.

For today, I ask for the willingness to hear my sponsor's message that guides me to freedom.

Promises Coming True

Great things are happening to me, as stated in the FAA promises, because I am participating in my own recovery. I am seeing things in a different light. I have a new understanding of life. I feel better with each day, and my decision-making abilities are improving. My thinking and clarity have improved beyond what I could have imagined.

I see the beauty in nature. I have become more adventurous. I try things that I would never have tried before abstinence, like hiking or roller skating. My discussions are not loud. I can talk calmly and can express my opinions serenely. I am able to sleep peacefully at night.

As I reflect on the great things happening in my life in recovery, I am grateful. I am experiencing the many miracles that FAA brings me. I am making meaningful friendships with other food addicts. I keep in mind that my primary purpose in FAA is to stay abstinent and to help other food addicts achieve abstinence.

For today, I believe that if I persevere, greater things will come.

Remaining Abstinent is a Choice

When I'm feeling negative, I can choose how to react. In my day, do I struggle with the hard times or turn them over to my Higher Power? When I need comfort, do I turn to food or to God?

When overwhelming emotions come into play, my old habit was to numb myself with sugar, flour, and wheat. I turned to food quickly and furiously without thinking about the consequences. However, after a binge, my pain and shame were not numbed. Instead, they were brought to new heights and I was brought to new lows.

With abstinence and a clear mind, I can now think through that first destructive bite before it leads to a binge. I can choose to deal with painful experiences and negative emotions in ways that nurture me, not numb me. I can reach for God and by doing so I reach for life.

For today, I choose to remain abstinent no matter what crisis invades my life.

Keeping to Our Purpose

Each group has but one primary purpose – to carry its message to the food addict who still suffers. (FAA Tradition Five)

We can understand the misery of food addiction because we have been there. We respond to the cry for help from a suffering food addict because our cries for help have been answered. We share our strength because we have been helped to find our own inner strength. We can offer hope because we now see our lives through eyes of hope.

Tradition Five keeps the fellowship on target. The groups don't take on more than their common experience with food addiction. FAA doesn't dilute the program by trying to cure any other ills or stray into paths of religion, psychology, or politics. We maintain unity by sharing the message of the Twelve Steps.

Sailing an uncharted sea, we drift unless we can set a course and head toward a destination. Tradition Five is the beacon that gives the fellowship its direction and goal.

For today, I ask God to preserve our precious FAA meetings.

The Gift of Laughter

Am I too serious? Am I so caught up in this thing called abstinence that I forget to stop along the way and enjoy my journey?

Food addiction is serious business. It robbed me of strength and energy. It bogged me down with feelings of guilt and shame. I didn't see a way out. Every day seemed a chore. All I could see as an answer was my warped pattern of addictive eating. I thought I had no choice.

In abstinence, I am given a whole world of choices. Through working the FAA program of recovery, the sky is the limit. Although this program of recovery is a serious one, I can laugh at the world and myself every now and then. It is therapeutic to have a good belly laugh. Silliness can be beneficial. Playing a game can be just the medicine I need to snap me out of a funk. Can I see the humor in some situations or do I mope around with a philosophy of gloom and doom? It is okay to let my hair down and have fun.

Think about it. God made ostriches and porcupines. Isn't it funny that God also made us? Help me to laugh again, but may I never forget how I once cried.

For today, I will see laughter and fun as God-given gifts that I can enjoy to the fullest.

Abstinence and Spirituality

Abstinence teaches us that spirituality is central to recovery. Ours is a faith-based journey. Growth is impossible without an ongoing relationship with our Higher Power. Getting food addiction out of the middle of the relationship makes it possible to develop the faith, hope, and trust required to face vulnerability and to ask for help. Humbly asking our Higher Power for help is just the beginning of the process. Next comes listening to, accepting, and acting on the guidance and encouragement offered.

Life is transformed as I learn to trust and surrender to the Higher Power of my understanding. I have come to believe that I am never alone. The emptiness inside has been filled with unconditional love. Today I open my heart and accept the love that is forever flowing in my life. Then I pass it on. In this way, the circle of love, trust, faith, and hope remains unbroken.

For today, I pray that my Higher Power removes any impediments that prevent me from fully surrendering to the FAA way of life.

Treating Myself With Love and Nurturing

In recovery, we learn new ways to treat ourselves. We now realize that our loving Higher Power provides us with pleasurable new opportunities that no longer include the toxins of sugar, wheat, and flour. Each day we can ask our Higher Power to guide us to new treats in our lives.

We can set aside a special soul-nurturing place in our homes where we commune with our Higher Power by listening and praying. We can give ourselves permission to allow open spaces of time in our schedules just to relax and reflect on the beauty that surrounds us. With the money that we once used for addictive food, we can now treat ourselves to the better-quality, nourishing food that we never thought we could afford. Or we can use that money to attend FAA retreats and the FAA convention.

We can enjoy a walk or bike ride with our friends. We can give ourselves permission to surround ourselves with nurturing people. We can start or end our day with a prayer of gratitude for a new lease on life.

For today, I ask my Higher Power to open my eyes to new treats that will benefit me.

Taking Responsibility

We are responsible for our well-being. In the past, we deluded ourselves into believing that others would (or should) take care of us. We were caught in the pity-pot trap. If circumstances made obtaining an abstinent meal difficult, then we blamed others, used the opportunity to stray into addictive eating, and opened the door to our disease.

Many a hard-earned lesson taught us that we are a vital thread in the fabric of humanity, as is each of our fellow human beings. Our needs are no more important than theirs are. Food addiction is our disease, and recovery is our responsibility.

Today, with guidance from our Higher Power, we take competent and loving care of ourselves. We meet the day prepared. Our first priority is preparing our food. We do not rely on anyone to do this for us. It is nice to have help from friends and family, but ultimately, it is our responsibility.

For today, I give thanks that I can take the steps necessary to ensure that my food needs are met and that my abstinence is secure.

Experiencing Unconditional Love

Admitted to God, to ourselves, and to another human being the exact nature of our wrongs. (FAA Step Five)

That first word – admitted – may stop us cold in our tracks. We come into this program being skilled at lying and creating our own version of the truth. Admitting anything wasn't part of our nature. When we stole candy, we denied any knowledge. When the leftover meatloaf for the next evening meal disappeared, we shrugged our shoulders. Denial became a way of life that gave birth to shame and guilt.

The taking of Step Five with our sponsor is the beginning of a feeling of unconditional love. We speak the truth to God, ourselves, and another human being. As each tear is shed, we begin to heal. Our sponsors share their stories with us and continue to teach us. And as we grow in the program by working the Twelve Steps, we find our real source of strength.

For today, I ask my Higher Power to remind me to love unconditionally as I am loved.

Experience, Strength and Hope

Each group has but one primary purpose - to carry its message to the food addict who still suffers. (FAA Tradition Five)

Tradition Five challenges us to keep our program single-minded. Our purpose is simple – to carry the message. FAA members meet to focus on their recovery through the practice of the Twelve Steps.

We are all able to smile and to listen. Maybe a troubled newcomer needs exactly this. We are careful to share our program, not to advise and not to urge decisions. We do not undertake emotional burdens nor sit in judgment.

As we grow in our understanding of the program, we learn compassion for the newcomer. Eventually we are able to let go of resentments that may be blocking our progress, preventing us from becoming the person we want to be.

As the pain and confusion in our life eases, we find we are prompted by gratitude to share what we have learned. Healing takes place at our meetings – healing of ourselves and of those who join us seeking the help that FAA offers.

For today, I will attend a meeting and welcome the newcomer who still suffers.

How I View My Abstinence

People often ask me how I gave up sugar, flour, wheat, and other addictive foods, implying that I have made some great sacrifice or that I must have a lot of willpower. I have not sacrificed anything nor do I have the willpower. Instead, I have the freedom of choice through the gift of abstinence.

I am a food addict. I cannot afford the luxury of fantasizing about the false imagery of joy I would receive from eating addictive foods. Through FAA, I now realize that my body chemistry created my addiction. I crossed the line from normal eater to addict long ago, and there is no going back. There is a solution with abstinent eating.

For today, I am thankful for the freedom I received with the gift of abstinence.

Doing My Part

Some days life is difficult and our emotions go off track. Our disease tells us to eat everything in sight. We may feel at such times that being a food addict in recovery is particularly tough, especially if we eat inappropriately. This behavior causes us shame, remorse, and frustration. We may feel that we are in a downward spiral.

Talking about our feelings can really help quiet our voracious disease. By confronting our fear, anger, and guilt, we don't feel as overwhelmed. We don't need to compensate for feelings of deprivation by bingeing.

Instead, we can nurture ourselves with meditation, asking for help from our Higher Power. We can read the literature, and call our sponsor. We follow our food plan and we stay abstinent. In this way, we do our part and let God do God's part in lifting our obsession with food.

For today, I take care of myself by practicing nurturing acts of love, knowing I am worth it.

Choosing the Right Attitude

Cutting vegetables, cleaning out the fridge, washing dishes, shopping for food that supports our abstinence, and cooking our meals can feel overwhelming. We may resent how much time we spend taking care of our needs. In the past, we may even have thrown up our hands and driven to the local convenience store for binge foods.

Recalling such memories can stop us in our tracks. We can recall how miserable we were and make a decision to choose a new attitude. We can ask ourselves, "What do I need right now?" The answer may be to rest, call a friend, or to write in our journal.

We no longer take our frustrations out on ourselves by bingeing. We have better choices. An attitude of gratitude can make a big difference in how we approach our program and our life. We reap many more benefits than the efforts we contribute.

For today, I give thanks for the spiritual practice of choosing the right attitude.

Reality of Abstinence

Some days I have to be gentler on myself. I need to rest. I need to reach out even more than usual or have some more quiet time alone. I am human. I have ups and downs. I feel well and happy sometimes and down, tired, and weary other times. I have periods of energy and periods of lethargy. I have days that are easy and days that are hard. I have days that I am hungry and days that I am not.

We all have difficulties, and what does it matter? When I was bingeing on sugar, flour, wheat, and volume, questioning "Why?" left me with the answer of "So what?" What matters is that I always have the program close by and I am committed to my abstinence. What matters is that I know that I am getting the nourishment that I need. Everything else is secondary. I always need to be hard on the addiction, but gentle on the addict.

When I am able to get past me, I can reach out to you. When I reach out and share my experience, strength, and hope, the healing happens. My strength and hope multiply when I share them with another food addict.

For today, I remain abstinent no matter what conditions I may face.

Recovery Begins With Me

In our old ways of thinking, we may have put barriers and conditions on where we could live in recovery. We may have thought that we needed near-perfect conditions to recover from our painful food addiction.

With abstinence, our thinking becomes clearer, and we can be honest. We ask the questions: If there were a meeting near my home, would that guarantee my abstinence? If I had a chef to prepare my meals, would I be ensured abstinence? Would making unlimited phone calls keep me abstinent? If I had a sponsor living next door, would I stay abstinent?

There is neither a perfect time nor perfect circumstances in which to recover. Today we take responsibility. Our actions include surrendering and asking our Higher Power for help with our recovery. We can do what needs doing. We can follow the FAA food plan, commit our food, and weigh and measure our meals. We can work the Steps of the program to keep us in the now and let go of our old, limiting ideas. We meet each challenge as it comes, and live in recovery today.

For today, I am responsible for my own recovery and take the actions required.

My Hero Has Arrived

I can recall reading stories, daydreaming, and praying for a hero to take care of my wants and needs, to respect me, to make me feel important, to rescue me. Today, I have found that hero. My hero is my Higher Power. As I remain abstinent, I can depend on myself and on my Higher Power to meet all my wants and needs. I enjoy good health, high spirits, and healthy ambitions. I recognize my talents and pursue them.

With abstinence, I feel love for myself. I take great care of my body, mind, and spirit. I have newfound self-respect. I am important not only to myself but also to other food addicts. I am a living example of how Food Addicts Anonymous and abstinence can give us back our lives.

For today, I am a testament to the hero that has been there for me all along – my Higher Power.

Looking at My Own Behavior

When I was active in my food addiction, I had no confidence in myself. I felt a great need to blame other people and other things for my out-of-control eating. I blamed my problems on my family, genetics, real or imagined abuse, finances, and work. I blamed God for not answering my prayers. Everything outside myself was at fault. Ironically, all the time I was blaming every one and every thing else, I was hating myself even more for what I thought was weakness. It became a vicious cycle: the more pain I was in, the more I had to blame someone or something else.

When I came into FAA, I was guided through the Steps. I was able to look at my behavior honestly and without shame. I was able to change the things I could, accept the things I could not change, and make amends wherever possible. I like the nicer, gentler person I have become.

For today, I take responsibility for what I say and do.

Accepting Options

"Pain   is   inevitable.   Suffering   is   optional."
-Anonymous

The disease of food addiction deceived me in so many ways before recovery. All my energy was spent searching for a way to avoid the pain in my life, using the escape promised me by food. As a result, I constantly suffered the misery of shame, failure, and hopelessness. The suffering was inevitable as long as I persisted in the belief that pain is optional and somehow could be avoided "if only...." I never realized that I had the power to choose or reject suffering.

Abstinence gives me the ability to accept the reality that life is sometimes painful and that I no longer need to struggle to avoid the pain. When I accept and embrace reality, the pain diminishes and I am free to move on.

For today, I will accept pain as another lesson in life.

In God's Hands

My Higher Power guides me no matter what I'm doing, no matter where I am. When I look back, I can see that even in the worst of my addiction, God was there for me. My drug of choice, food, did not drive God away. If anything, God held me tighter, full of compassion for my suffering. Nonetheless, I could not perceive this. I felt alone and abandoned. I felt unlovable and worthless.

Abstinence and recovery have not made me more worthy as a human being, nor of God's love; instead they have lifted the veil of darkness, revealing to me that I am precious.

My joy comes not in attaining God's love, but in recognizing that it is with me always. My mind is clear of doubt, fear, and the fog of addictive foods, and so I am able to perceive and embrace this truth.

For today, I am grateful that I may fully experience the joy of living in God's love and light.

Humility

Narcissus fell in love with his own reflection, which he believed was another person. He wasted his life vainly seeking his perfect self, which of course he never found.

Like Narcissus, we addicts strived to attain nothing less than perfection. When we inevitably fell short, we berated ourselves.

In surrendering to recovery, we begin the process of fully awakening to reality, of accepting life on life's terms. We come to accept ourselves as fallible human beings, not as mythical gods of peerless beauty, intellect, and power.

Today we are a little more humble and a lot happier. Humility has come to us not by searching for it but by acquiring it. And today we know that humility is a gift.

Our search for our perfect selves has come to an end. May God help us to see ourselves as the perfectly imperfect beings that we are, so that we can rest in the moment and experience joy.

For today, I pray to humbly receive any success or progress as a gift divinely sent. My sole ambition is to know and do God's will.

Perseverance

The disease of food addiction inflicts severe trauma on the body, mind, and soul. Healing takes much time and considerable effort. Inevitably, we all face obstacles, discouragement, and frustrations.

For many of us, getting abstinent is the greatest challenge. For others, staying abstinent is the greatest struggle. Still others surrender with relative ease and achieve stable abstinence but resist emotional or spiritual growth.

Regardless of the category that we fall into, each of us can recover. No obstacle is so great that our Higher Power cannot remove it. The key is perseverance. When frustrated or discouraged, those who ultimately find freedom from this disease trust in the process and persevere.

Having learned to trust and persevere, we find that subsequent trials pass more easily. Trust and perseverance are rewarded with a sense of the FAA Promises coming true for us. We gladly do whatever it takes.

For today, I pray for the willingness to persevere and to trust that God will see me through.

It's Easier to Stay Abstinent

Surely it is easier to stay abstinent than it is to get abstinent. I just have to look back at all my failed attempts to begin this abstinent lifestyle. So many times I was left asking myself WHY, when my intentions had been so clear and honest. Little did I know that I was powerless to follow through with my true desire – to just eat sensibly.

Over time, I came to realize that just wanting to stay abstinent didn't give me the power to be abstinent. To stay abstinent, I first had to surrender completely. As I listen to others' struggles, I am reminded that I cannot do this alone. Left to my own devices, I will relapse.

Once I reached the conclusion that I must surrender completely and let other people into my life, my Higher Power was manifested. This started with the simplest of prayers: "God, help me be abstinent today!" and was followed by another very simple prayer: "Thank you for this gift of abstinence today!" The simple prayers of a child – "please" and "thank you – was all that was needed."

This complete surrender has brought joy, peace, and serenity into my life.

For today, I cherish the gift of abstinence and I will go to whatever lengths are necessary to preserve it.

Progress Not Perfection

Progress, not perfection, is the key to my serenity. Knowing that I'll never be perfect is okay as long as I keep working on the areas of my life that I would like to change.

When our sponsors told us that we could ask God to remove our defects of character, we may have thought that this recovery work would be a snap. However, the FAA book calls recovery a lengthy process. I continue to utilize the tools of recovery that are available to me and continue to progress in recovery.

What really matters is my willingness to change. Continuous abstinence keeps my tool belt handy and keeps me moving in the right direction.

For today, I stay in the solution. I accept myself with all my imperfections and continue to recover.

My Life as a Portrait

Just as each stroke of a paintbrush adds to the completion of a picture, so each step that we learn to take in FAA helps us complete the pattern of our lives. We may make mistakes as we learn to work the Steps, but as we grow in confidence, so do our skills and willingness to learn.

When we have completed our picture, we can look at our handiwork with satisfaction and confidence. Each step we take in recovery gives us satisfaction, because we begin to see the tattered pieces of our lives coming together into a beautiful portrait. Confidence comes in knowing that we have been taking each step abstinently.

For today, I use my sponsor, the Steps, and the tools to inspire and help me create the canvas of my life, free of food addiction.

Self-Centered

As a food addict, I am a very self-centered person. In recovery, I check my motives and try to think about what I am going to say and do. I consider how it will affect the other person and if what I am going to say is helpful or hurtful. This is hard work! It is like being in school every day! I like it though – it keeps me on my toes and from growing complacent.

By applying the Steps to my life, I become self-caring. I no longer have the need to be right, the center of attention, or abusive to others. I have been acting self-centered for many years. This behavior is not what I want to exhibit. The longer I am abstinent, the more God expects of me and the more I expect of myself.

For today, I think before I speak and ask God to remove my shortcomings.

Service is a Form of Love

You are sitting next to me. My eyes are drawn to you in this room full of strangers. I try not to stare. We sit in small, straight-backed chairs and you look so miserable. I try to catch your glance. Will you talk to me? I search for your eyes. I look. I question, "Is anyone in there?"

You are my brother or sister who still suffers. I want to lovingly reach over and tap on your shoulder, hopefully easing you out of your stupor. I want to tell you, "There is a solution." But all I can do is silently, passionately pray for your recovery.

Your suffering is my suffering. Your disease is my disease. When you are ready, I will be present for you. I will take your hand, and together we will travel this road from addiction to sanity, from pain to gratitude. This is service.

I am just like you. I have found a solution that I want to share with you.

For today, I remember my brokenness so that I will continue to help another suffering food addict.

What is Clarity?

I keep hearing about clarity. The old-timers at meetings mention it when they share. What is this thing called clarity? Whatever it is, I want it! I long for it and patiently wait for it to mysteriously appear.

In the meantime, I cling to the freedom found in honesty. I go to meetings, I read, I write, and I make phone calls. I suspect that clarity will arrive, perhaps when I least expect it. I trust the promises of the program. Isn't that in itself already a little piece of clarity?

The more I stay in the solution, the more I am able to see and accept my potential as well as my shortcomings. It is becoming easier for me to make good choices, because my mind isn't fogged with addictive foods. I am having better relationships with others because I am allowing them the dignity of being who and what they are.

Clarity may be slow to come, but I think I'm getting it. I understand what it means to have clarity.

For today, I work on my recovery and look forward to preserving the gift of clarity that comes as a result.

Choosing to Stay in Recovery

*Sharing our experience, strength, and hope with others
allows us to recover from this disease one day at a time.*
(<u>Food Addicts Anonymous</u>, *Definition of Abstinence*)

We may have considered gastric bypass or a
weight-loss spa, especially when we continued to be
humiliated by our bingeing. Hope was not in our
vocabulary. We had tried everything.

Somehow we dragged ourselves to our first FAA
meeting. We listened, and we were amazed that there
were others who ate as we did and who found an
answer. We were filled with hope. Our prayers
were answered, not with a bypass or a spa, but
with something that gives us so much more – the
fellowship of FAA. In this fellowship, others know our
feelings and shame, because they have had the same
experiences…and they wanted to share the solution
with us.

We become hopeful that we will get what we need
in the FAA rooms. Recovery is evident in the bright and
loving faces of those who so willingly share their truths
with me.

*For today, I give thanks that others have shown me a
solution.*

It Quit Working

There was a time when I didn't think I could get through the hard times, the emotional roller coasters of my life, without bingeing. I needed to eat, and I did. It wasn't pretty, I wasn't healthy, and I was definitely digging my grave. I continually gained weight, but kept eating more and more.

When I came to FAA, I started sharing about how scared I was to put down the addictive substances. I was afraid that I would not be able to deal with my emotions. I just kept talking about that fear and eventually, although I was scared, I made the decision to start committing my food to another food addict.

I had to "face the fear and do it anyway." I also had to accept that where I had been was where I needed to be at the time, but that I didn't need to be there anymore.

Action followed my decision. I went to meetings, I got a sponsor, I kept committing my food, and I learned how to practice the FAA program. By using the time-tested tools, I am free to live my life in a sane and healthy manner.

For today, I ask my Higher Power to grant me the gift of abstinence for another 24 hours.

Abstinence Comes First

When I stopped eating addictive foods, abstinence became the most important thing in my life. My recovery had to come before everything else in my life in order for me to have a life. I had to decide that I come first, which means that my recovery and abstinence come first. No matter what!

I understand the importance of staying abstinent, listening to my sponsor and taking suggestions, and reading all food labels and purchasing nothing that contains addictive substances. I keep my cupboards clear of any foods that are not on my food plan. I do not listen to the disease when it says that I can start my abstinence tomorrow. I do not eat addictive foods. I abstain from my binge foods. I rest when I am tired. I start now, in the present. If I don't start now, I may never start at all.

In the past I had admitted that I was a food addict, but I had not opened my heart to accept the gift of unconditional abstinence, one day at a time. Today I am an addict who is experiencing the joy of recovery; I thank God sincerely for saving my life with this program. FAA is truly a gift.

For today, I cherish my unconditional abstinence as a gift from God.

Freedom Not Perfection

Were entirely ready to have God remove all these defects of character. (FAA Step Six)

We may like the very trait our sponsor views as a defect. "That's just me," we protest. We don't get ready to change until we see that a characteristic is contributing to the unmanageability in our lives. Before we get to that point, we must overcome self-justification.

We're often fearful that in giving up a characteristic, even something as destructive as perfectionism, we are losing a precious part of ourselves. Our desire for perfectionism, which has extended to demanding perfection in others as well, can make us self-righteous and unforgiving.

The searching and fearless moral inventory of the Fourth Step was the beginning of an honest look at who we are. In admitting the nature of our wrongs in Step Five, we identified elements of our character that are causing us pain. Now, in Step Six, we cut through self-deception and become entirely ready to give up behaviors that have been troubling us.

For today, I ask God to continue to lead me toward freedom and not perfection.

Humility and Sincerity

In Step Five, we admit to God, to ourselves, and to another human being the exact nature of our wrongs. I acknowledge and admit my wrongs to God. I acknowledge my truth and I share it with another human being. I find someone who is trustworthy, with whom I can fully share what's in my head and in my heart.

In Step Six, we are entirely ready to have God remove all our defects of character. This is where my transformation begins. Step Six frees me from the lies that I have held on to for so many years, and my truth begins to set me free. My sincerity allows God to make me aware of my shortcomings. Humility allows me to realize that I can't do this alone and that there is a Power greater than myself who will help me.

Only God has the power to remove my character defects. Through abstinence I can continue my recovery. By following suggestions and staying on the food plan, my thinking gets clearer. I attend FAA meetings because I need help. I am here to get well. I know that my Higher Power has a better plan for me.

The ultimate is knowing God is doing for me what I couldn't do for myself. God loves me too much to leave me where I was.

For today, I share how grateful I am for the rooms of FAA and for all who keep me on track by sharing their experience, strength, and hope.

Emotional Stability

Emotional stability is a blessed gift of recovery.

When we experience feelings of anxiety or melancholy, we do not need to pick up our binge foods, which will eventually cause us to spiral out of control. Instead of using food to handle depression, anger, rage, and confusion, we can take some quiet time, pray, reach out to a fellow food addict, journal, or read recovery literature. We have options today that enable us to touch our center, our true self.

We trust that we can be sane and free. Food temporarily made us oblivious to the pain of unresolved issues. But now that we are centered and secure, we are ready to look at our life, accept it, and embrace it fully. We are ready for freedom.

For today, I ask God to keep me ever aware that I have options. I am no longer rendered helpless by strong emotions.

Asset or Defect?

Were entirely ready to have God remove all these defects of character. (FAA Step Six)

I have never let go of a character defect without claw marks. I used to rationalize that my character defects were in fact virtues. I would tell myself that, yes, I am shy and withdrawn, but that's because I am sensitive and misunderstood. Or yes, I lie, but people cannot be trusted with the truth: I am not deceitful, just a diplomat.

I defended my defects and even exalted them as traits that made me special. I was very attached to them and reluctant to acknowledge them as shortcomings that made my life needlessly difficult. I could not imagine who I would be without them.

In truth, my character defects are little demons that grab a part of my personality and soul and prevent me from being the person God truly intended me to be. Thus, surrendering my character defects never diminishes me. The closer I come to living as God wills me to live, the easier and more joyful my life becomes.

For today, I pray that God will keep me open and ready to let go of my character defects, so that in God's time they can be lifted.

Postponing Instant Gratification

I am a food addict and I want what I want when I want it. That was the basis many times for my eating. I saw something and then I ate it with little thought of the consequences. I knew if it was gooey and sticky and sweet, I would get a quick high – but I would pay an enormous price later.

Many times I acted impulsively. I acted without regard for the possible ramifications. I acted on an impulse. And the results were never good.

Today I weigh and measure my food and also weigh and measure the pros and cons of any action I take. I look closely at the end product, not just what pleasure I can get out of some food or some behavior immediately. This keeps me on the right track physically, emotionally, and spiritually. Before I act, I think.

For today, I think through the impulsive thought before I act. My abstinence is well worth the extra effort.

God's Passenger

When I was in the throes of my disease, I was driven by obsession; the obsession to hide, sneak, lie, or steal my binge foods. My mind-numbing substances drove me to literally be a danger on the road as I navigated the streets and freeways of my community drunk on refined carbohydrates. With a mind distracted by what my next binge food would be, I often drove right past my intended destination.

In abstinence, I am no longer a menace to others or myself on the road. I am alert, careful, and considerate. I am a grateful passenger on the journey of life. God directs, I drive, and abstinence clears the way.

For today, I seek God and abstinence as my constant companion on the road called life.

Living in the Solution

Most of us find that physical recovery comes to us before we can begin to heal emotionally and spiritually. We remain abstinent, and then, to maintain our abstinence, we work on healing emotionally and spiritually.

Recovery through FAA is progressive. Just as our addiction was progressive, so too is our recovery. There is no end. We continue to grow and develop throughout our lives. We can choose to follow spiritual principles, which contribute to our emotional healing, or we can choose to go back to addictive foods to escape reality.

We find that by maintaining all three legs of the stool (physical, emotional, and spiritual growth), we stay balanced. And balance is an integral part of recovery.

For today, I abstain from addictive substances and work the Steps so that I may stay balanced.

Who Has the Eraser?

Two of the FAA slogans are "Let go and let God" and "Failing to plan is planning to fail." These seem to be in opposition to each other. How can I let go if I am busy planning? The answer is simpler than it seems: I need to plan for those things I can control.

Is there abstinent food available for my meals?

Do I need to pack a meal in case I can't get home for a meal and abstinent food isn't available?

Is there room for balance and moderation in my day? Work? Recovery? Play? Self-care?

Then I remember that my plans are written in pencil and that God holds the eraser. God will reveal the results of my plans as my day unfolds. Perhaps God has a very different plan in mind for me today. Living in serenity, I will accept the plans that God reveals.

For today, I plan a day that supports my physical, emotional, and spiritual recovery. I leave the results up to God.

Moving Forward

After taking Steps Four and Five, I thought that Step Six would be easy. Yes, I was ready for God to remove these shortcomings, so why wasn't I serene and calm? I was abstinent, but I still wasn't happy.

I looked again at Step Six, "Were entirely ready to have God remove these defects of character." Okay, if God removed my defect of laziness, I would have to get busy. Was I ready for that? If God removed my stubbornness, was I ready to be cooperative? If my feelings were hurt, what would I do to replace my pouting? What will replace these traits in me?

Instead of having faith and trust in whatever was in store for me, I kept thinking that I could figure it out on my own. Then I realized that I wasn't ready. I needed to go back to Steps Two and Three again. I was trying to work the Steps on my own, trying to sort out which character defects I wanted to give up and which ones I wanted to keep.

Only when I am completely ready to have my character defects removed and believe that whatever replaces them will be good for me can I really take this Sixth Step.

For today, I let God be in charge of what character defects need to be removed.

Opening the Door to Acceptance

We may have believed that life couldn't be fun without sugary desserts or bread and butter. When we first walked into FAA, we may have thought that the people there were crazy for abstaining from sugar, flour, and wheat. Once we get a sponsor, we learn that we can ask for help from a Higher Power to relieve our desire to eat addictive foods. We learn the value of honesty, open-mindedness, and willingness. Most important, we learn that food addiction is a biochemical disease.

At first, fear may keep us abstinent. We may have trouble taking Step Two, at which point our sponsor points out that we don't have to believe that a power greater than ourselves can restore us to sanity – we only have to be willing to believe. It's that simple. We don't have to force ourselves to believe in something; all that is required is willingness.

For today, I gratefully acknowledge that God often speaks through other people and that FAA works if I work it.

Surrender Control

Letting go of my obsessive need to control is very difficult for me. When I decide to ask God to remove my shortcomings, I may want to control how and when it happens. What a paradox! I am used to calling all the shots, so when asking God for help, I may dictate a timetable for when I am ready to have these shortcomings removed.

But God does things in God's time, not in my time. Humility is vital in my surrender. I must be willing to learn and to wait. I must be willing to be like clay in the hands of a potter. The clay does not give orders to the potter nor argue or complain.

When I put my life in God's hands, God reshapes it. It is only in humility that I can accept this reshaping and accept the change. God is a master artisan, making me beautiful and effective. I just need to get out of the way.

For today, I ask God to gently reshape me as I rest patiently in God's hands.

Open to Change

Today I view character defects as mini-addictions. They are little symptoms of the disease. Gossip and judgment, for instance. Why would I gossip or criticize anyone?

I may have prayed for years, asking God to remove this character defect. So why do I gossip? Does it make me feel better about myself? Or, in the long run, worse?

I eat to feel better, but then the remorse and guilt make me feel so much worse. I have to do it all again. The bingeing then becomes the cure for the pain and the cause of the pain, all rolled into one.

I came to this program and made a decision to learn a new way of living. If I can see my character defects as mini-addictions, I may become entirely ready to have God remove them.

For today, I ask God to direct my life and release me from my character defects.

I've Earned My Seat

I have a right to be in Food Addicts Anonymous. My journey was long, hard, and painful. It seems to have taken forever for me to walk into these rooms. I have paid the enormous price of admission in emotional, physical, and spiritual terms to be here. Now that I am here, I do not wish to leave.

But how do I stay put? How do I increase my chances of not leaving? There are many, many tools of abstinence. One tool is affirming my right to be in FAA and my right to be at a meeting, whatever form that meeting might take. Maybe I have little to say and choose to listen, or instead prefer to share the intimate details of a problem with a trusted friend or sponsor. At a time like that, I am merely claiming my seat. I am acknowledging my presence as a food addict. I am letting others know that I am here. I am showing the newcomers that it is safe to choose whatever I feel like sharing. In the rooms of FAA, there is no one to judge me but myself. My seat is comfortable.

For today, I am claiming my seat in Food Addicts Anonymous. It sure feels good to be home.

Maintaining Abstinence While Traveling

The planet is a safe and lovely place. The greatest impediment to my recovery seems to be myself. If I am using the tools to help me stay fit spiritually, I can abstain even in the strangest of places. But, if I am not abstinent, I'm vulnerable in my own kitchen.

While traveling I can stay in a youth hostel dormitory in Paris or in a 4-star hotel in Moscow. I can ask where to find fruits and vegetables and can learn how to say, "No sugar" in any language. I can call ahead when going on a cruise.

It is my responsibility to be mindful of my own triggers, and to not get too hungry, angry, lonely, or tired. I have to ask for what I need and deserve. This can mean weighing and measuring in an unfamiliar place, calling my sponsor or attending a Twelve-Step meeting, even if it is not an FAA meeting. I can remember that I am always an addict wherever I go and that I have special needs that I must take care of. I can honor myself by acknowledging my powerlessness over my food addiction.

For today, I am responsible for my abstinence no matter where I am.

Letting Go of Character Defects

In sharing the exact nature of our wrongs with another human being and with God, we see that indulging in negative actions has kept us from having positive relationships, especially in our relationship with God.

With the help of our sponsor, we find that we no longer need to hold on to the character defects that at one time in our lives may have served us. We learn that it is better to love than be loved, to understand than to be understood, and to give comfort rather than to be comforted. Little by little, our character defects are removed as we continue to work the Steps.

For today, I seek to love, comfort, and understand others.

Day One

We often hear our fellow addicts who are struggling declare that they are back to Day One. We may have thought that Day One was synonymous with "You failed."

But let's reexamine Day One. It is a glorious day. It is certainly far preferable to Day Zero. Just one day can make all the difference, and the moment we stop eating sugar, flour, and wheat, we are abstinent.

Our first day of abstinence can begin at any moment. It need not begin at midnight or the next morning. The day has not been ruined. We begin Day One at the moment that we become willing to accept the gift of abstinence.

We can abstain from addictive foods for one 24-hour period. One day is all we need, and that day is today. We need never return to Day One, because we have never really left it. Today is always Day One.

For today, I pray that I will value my current abstinence as the only abstinence I'll ever need.

We Only Need to Be Ready

Were entirely ready to have God remove all these defects of character. (FAA Step Six)

Step Six requires us to stop struggling. It tells us that it is time to acknowledge that we need help. Having gone through Steps Four and Five, we are aware of our defects of character. Perhaps pride and feelings of superiority or the habit of judging others is blocking the way to true serenity. Perhaps feelings of deep resentment, envy, or self-pity keep us in turmoil.

All that Step Six requires is becoming ready. We don't have to achieve change immediately. We can work on our attitude and pray about it. We can think it over and see that our lives become less troublesome when we rid ourselves of destructive habits.

Step Six tells us to relax. We don't have to do it all alone. We can reflect. We can turn to our Higher Power with confidence. And once we become entirely ready, we can know that we will feel great relief, like heading into a shower after exercising. We emerge refreshed, shining, and ready.

We affirm to our Higher Power that we are ready to have our defects removed. We continue to stay in close contact with our Higher Power.

For today, I allow room for God to work in my life, making it possible for wonderful changes to take place.

Looking to a New Higher Power

In active addiction, food was my higher power. It was what I turned to daily as a source of strength and comfort. I especially sought it in times of sorrow or trouble, although I also binged in times of celebration. Food was a false god that shadowed my days. Its darkness could mask my feelings, but it could not show me how to live. I was lost, and neither my own efforts nor any human power could relieve me of this unholy dependence, but God could, and did.

My new Higher Power is a God of my understanding who lovingly guides me along the sunlit path of recovery. I may fall along the way, but I know where to turn when this happens, even when feelings of hopelessness overwhelm me. I trust that what God has awakened in me will continue to grow, unless I choose otherwise.

When the food tempts me, I know that I am losing sight of my Higher Power. When my spiritual perspective blurs, I begin easing God out of my life by reclaiming fear or resentment, and attempt to control circumstances or the people around me. And then addictive food, my false god, insidiously moves back into focus.

For today, I pray for strength, to maintain a clear spiritual vision of life, so that I look to food only to sustain and nourish me.

Quit the Debating Society

Some, with experience in recovery, have pointed out that an overriding reason for finding a power greater than ourselves, is to introduce us to humility, to help us understand that we are NOT the ultimate authority. (<u>Food Addicts Anonymous</u>, *Some Thoughts on Spirituality*)

Before finding FAA, many of us found recovery from other substances in other Twelve Step programs, but we were not willing to surrender addictive foods as readily.

When we got an FAA sponsor, we found ourselves holding on to our own opinions about food. We may have argued for certain health foods as part of our breakfast. When told that these foods were not on the food plan, we may have felt self-will rearing its ugly head. After all, we were unique!

We often have to remind ourselves that our best thinking got us here. We look at the miserable pit we had dug for ourselves and decide to quit the debating society. We become willing to do what we are told. We are no longer the ultimate authority.

Recovery works through the Twelve Step process when we are honest and when we surrender our will. We trust that our Higher Power will do for us what we were never able to do for ourselves.

For today, I surrender to the process of recovery in order to live life to the fullest.

Extra Food is Not The Answer

When we get abstinent from sugar, flour, and wheat, and work the Twelve Steps, we are ready to deal with life on life's terms and appreciate all the joys of abstinence. But, are there times when extra food is still used as a coping tool? When we eat extra food – even food that is on our food plan – to deal with life or feelings, we're still putting food between us and our Higher Power. We're still using food to deal with emotional or spiritual needs. We know all too well that extra food never fills us emotionally or spiritually. Instead, it blocks our growth as spiritual beings.

When we stop using extra food as a way to cope, we are free to experience the joys of abstinence. Only then can we know true freedom from our food addiction. Only then can we grow as spiritual beings, reaching for our Higher Power, not food, no matter what life brings us.

For today, I choose to seek my Higher Power and not extra food.

Food Is Not My Higher Power

God could not be #1 in my life until I surrendered my will and my life over to God's care. The grip of addiction kept everything subject to the addiction's overwhelming power. In recovery, I give God the steering wheel and sit peacefully and comfortably in the back seat.

Admitting my powerlessness is the most difficult part of this process. Like learning to walk, I commit to taking baby steps until I feel safe and secure. I surrender to the food plan without trying to manipulate it. The daily commitment to a changed life is one step at a time, one day at a time, and sometimes one minute at a time. Giving myself over to my Higher Power releases the stranglehold of my addiction. I find peace in the comfort of this new relationship.

Does abstinence bring about a relationship with a Power greater than myself or does a Power greater than myself bring about abstinence? I am not certain, but I know that I need both.

For today, I seek to improve my conscious contact with God.

Honoring Tradition Six

An FAA group ought never endorse, finance, or lend the FAA name to any related facility or outside enterprise, lest problems of money, property, and prestige divert us from our primary purpose. (FAA Tradition Six)

Desire for power and prestige is the opposite of a spiritual aim. Therefore, Tradition Six warns against engaging in outside enterprises, which can lead to preoccupation with material things.

On a group level, problems brought about by owning money and property could ruin the spiritual basis of our program. On a personal level, members who find themselves receiving recognition for their service work or length of abstinence may need to reevaluate their motives by regularly taking a personal inventory.

We can carry the message of FAA only when we are humble enough to know that we are messengers and that, in a sense, we are still beginners in the spiritual journey laid out in the Twelve Steps. All that we have to offer to others is our experience, strength, and hope.

By honoring this Tradition, the FAA groups will remain spiritual, not material.

For today, I remember that this is a spiritual, not a material program.

From Me to We

"We will be able to listen with empathy to other's suffering." (<u>Food Addicts Anonymous</u>, *The Process of Recovery*)

While in the active phase of my food addiction, I was focused, for the most part, on myself. Having the constant dialogue going on in my head about my next food fix or how I wasn't going to binge again, I had no energy to empathize with others. I wasn't a selfish person, just a person in disease.

As I recover and work with a sponsor who listens to me and accepts me, I feel loved. As a result, when newcomers share their feelings of hopelessness, I can listen with love and empathy.

Empathy is different than sympathy. Sympathy says, "Although I haven't experienced what you have, I am sorry for your situation." Empathy says, "I've traveled this road before. I understand. I've had those feelings too. I care. I will listen."

I want to be present to empathize with other food addicts so that we can all grow stronger in our recovery.

For today, I listen with empathy to another food addict.

Working Toward Acceptance

"We will no longer be judgmental about everyone we meet." (<u>Food Addicts Anonymous</u>, *The Process of Recovery*)

Each day in recovery, as we learn more about ourselves and about what valuable people we are, we become less and less judgmental about others.

As we grow in recovery, we find that our Higher Power helps us to live a free, useful life; our thinking becomes clearer and we are more open to seeing our true worth. We continue to keep the focus on ourselves and begin to have a better self-image.

We no longer project our old dark stuff onto others; instead, we reflect kindness and goodness. We accept others as they are and where they are. We realize that we are all children of God, and God is not finished with us.

For today, I focus my attention on giving only loving feedback and recognize that I am a work in progress.

Taking the Extra Time to Think

When I am anxious, angry, or uneasy, I can say the Serenity Prayer to calm me down. Doing this helps me to stay in today and refrain from projecting a situation into the future or dredging up past scenarios.

Calming down with the Serenity Prayer also allows me to take a quick inventory of the situation and see if I owe any apologies. I need to recognize when I've said or done something wrong. When I let the person involved know that I regret my actions, our relationship can get stronger. Taking a moment to stop, think, and act in a mature fashion is a gift of recovery.

In some perverse way, I may have enjoyed arguments at one time. I can no longer afford to go that route. If I allow myself to be too wound up over any situation, I run the risk of turning to my drug of choice – my binge foods. I no longer need to jump to my disease's command.

For today, I use the Serenity Prayer to give me time to think instead of react.

Living Again

Before recovery from this disease, I thought that I was living, but I wasn't, really. It was more like sleepwalking through life. I may have looked successful on the outside, but it was just a facade. Inside I was dead and I didn't even know it. I was going through the motions of life, but I had no spirit. I was living to eat and hating myself more and more with each day that passed and each pound that was added.

My disease told me lie after lie, and I was so miserable.

Even when I heard about recovery, I wanted to run from it. I didn't want to surrender. I don't know where I got the courage to even try. I was told to do it just for today and that is how I started.

Today, living in reality means doing the next right thing. My life may not be perfect, but if I am living in the present, it is good. I know that I am good enough and that feelings will pass. I do not have to have all the answers. I do not have to fix and take care of everyone. I just have to take care of me and be present for my family, friends, and coworkers.

I am not a number on a scale or a clothing size. I put my recovery before all else in my life, or I will be right back among the living dead.

For today, I cherish the reality in my recovery. I will not trade it for anything.

Eating Does Not Help

Uncertainty is hard for a food addict. We must practice letting go of what we cannot control. What will be will be.

Thankfully, we don't have to eat over the anxiety that uncertainty taps into. Will eating make the future more certain? Yes, in some ways life in active addiction was very predictable. We could depend on misery, shame, isolation, and many other negative reactions. Eating may have served to counter anxiety, but only at the price of our health and active participation in life. So the alternative to living with a little uncertainty is not so bad.

What will be will be.

For today, I trust in God enough to turn over what I cannot control, to remain present even in the face of uncertainty, and to let life gently flow.

Patience With Recovery

Recovery seems to have a variety of spiritual paths. Our members all come to FAA at various stages of spiritual and emotional growth. Some of us came through the doors and gave up sugar, flour, and wheat, never to eat them again. Others of us struggled for months to gain abstinence. Some of us, no matter how long we have tried, have not received the gift of consistent back-to-back abstinence.

Others of us began to work the Steps after our very first FAA meeting. We may have had difficulty letting go of our character defects. Wherever we fall on the spectrum of recovery, we learn that it is unwise to compare ourselves with others.

It doesn't matter where we fall on this spectrum. We can ask our Higher Power to help us gain insight and acceptance about our situation. We need to be patient with our recovery process. We must remember that as our disease is progressive, so is recovery. All of us have only today for our abstinence.

For today, I accept myself no matter what and pray for the insight I need to move forward.

Trusting Maintenance

When my Higher Power brought me to recovery for food addiction, it was such a gift. In the beginning, it was difficult to let go of old habits, especially excessive exercise. I had a great deal of fear of gaining weight.

Gradually, by working the program and continuing to listen to my sponsor and others in recovery, I began to trust. I trusted that I would be okay. I did not need to be obsessive and in control of everything. I began to find a more balanced life. I trusted that my Higher Power did not bring me this far to abandon me, and my faith grew and grew. I turned my will and my life, including my body, over to the care of my Higher Power.

Today I exercise in moderation. If I have thoughts of working out beyond what I have agreed on with my sponsor, I talk to my sponsor, just as I would if I had thoughts of overeating or restricting. It usually means there are other issues going on that I need to look at.

FAA has brought me balance in all areas of my life. I am no longer driven to control everything. It's amazing that by putting down addictive foods one day at a time, the moderate exercise follows and the gifts just keep on coming.

For today, I ask my Higher Power to remind me that the scale is no longer the measuring stick by which I measure my life.

Learning to Say No

Abstinence in FAA is teaching me how to take care of myself. One of the best ways I can do that is by learning to say NO to unhealthy people, places, and things.

There are people who do not understand food addiction. They may intentionally or unintentionally be undermining my program. They may offer me food that is not on my food plan. I can say NO to them.

There are places that may set off cravings or set me up to associate pleasant memories with unhealthy foods. This is a risk I cannot afford to take. I can say NO to them.

There are things that I can no longer keep around my home. I cannot risk losing my abstinence by allowing foods that are hazardous to my recovery to be around me. I can say NO to them, too.

By asserting my God-given right to say NO, I am saying YES to me.

For today, I safely say NO to anything I feel is a danger to my abstinence.

Asking in Humility

The first six Steps lead us to want to free ourselves from the past and from destructive emotions. When we were immersed in eating addictive foods with feelings of inferiority, remorse, anger, resentment, and retaliation, we closed ourselves off from people and from our Higher Power. Now, in being ready to let go of our shortcomings, we are able to listen and to be healed.

Having acknowledged a Power greater than ourselves, we can make contact and ask to be restored to health and serenity. What do we ask? We ask to become free of that heavy burden of negative emotion and long-standing defects of character. How do we ask? We ask with complete faith that something good will happen. We trust that the good within us will be recovered as we improve. Whom do we ask? We ask the God of our understanding.

As we ask humbly, we are discarding arrogant pride. We are letting go of the arrogance of denying our need to change. We are conquering the pride that kept us self-righteous. We are overcoming the fear that kept us locked in. We are becoming open. Our heart is lightened. There is a spring in our step.

For today, I ask God to give me the spiritual help that brings me inner peace.

Strengthened by Faith

Humbly asked God to remove our shortcomings. (FAA Step Seven)

When I became convinced that I was indeed powerless over my food addiction and that my life had become unmanageable, Step Seven held the key to more freedom and growth in recovery.

Some of us had gone very far along the road of distorted thinking before reaching out for help. We spent years in self-inflicted pain because of our obsession with addictive foods. Then we found the program, stayed abstinent, and took the Steps. Strengthened by faith, we trusted God to help us. We learned to forego our will for God's will.

Spent of energy and despairing, we tried asking our Higher Power to remove the shortcomings that blocked our vision and prevented our growth. We asked humbly because we knew we were dependent on God for progress; humbly also because we were forced to accept our limitations and defeats.

Then we learned that humility is not self-abasement. Instead, humility is being honest, facing reality, and remaining teachable.

For today, I strive to feel the freedom that Step Seven brings.

Avoiding Relapse

FAA offers a healthy and satisfying food plan that takes away our cravings. We also receive the gift of a warm and understanding group of people to support us. Meetings, literature, and the 12 life-changing Steps support us as well.

Food addiction is a powerful disease and may call to us occasionally. It may call to us when we feel angry, sad, or hurt. It may call to us when we want to celebrate with food or when people ask us why we follow such a restrictive diet. It may lead us to question whether we really are food addicts. We may find ourselves thinking, "Maybe this time I can handle small amounts of sugar, flour, and wheat."

Some of us took back our will many times and tried to control our out-of-control eating. We may have believed that this time it would be different. It never is. It only gets worse when we pick up addictive foods.

We have a chronic, progressive, and fatal disease. FAA offers a solution that frees us from food addiction with the help of our Higher Power, our sponsor, and the tools of the FAA program.

For today, I ask my Higher Power to guide me through my bleak periods of recovery.

Celebrations

Since I found FAA and a new way of living, there is much in my life to celebrate. I have been released from the bondage of food. My life is no longer centered on food, what to eat, where to hide it, how to hide the wrappers, and the weight gain.

Now my life is centered on a Higher Power who is a loving, nurturing source of wisdom that guides me to a happy, peaceful life. I am able to be present in my life and enjoy the beauty that surrounds me.

As I work the Steps, my character defects are removed from me. I grow and become the person I was always meant to be: free, useful, and happy.

I celebrate this growth and acknowledge the changes in my life. I take the time to recognize the changes in the inner me.

For today, I recognize the growth I have achieved in FAA, and I celebrate my new way of living.

Tool Kit of Recovery

As I start this God-given day abstinently, I realize this is truly the first day of the rest of my life. Before I abstained from sugar, wheat, and flour, the disease consumed my days. I tried countless ways to control my food intake, to no avail.

I use the tools of this program to focus my mind on recovery rather than on abusing my body. I do whatever it takes to avoid foods not on the FAA food plan. I prepare and measure my meals and call my sponsor. I turn over to my Higher Power anything that I cannot handle. I do not pick up, no matter what.

Abstinence is a daily reprieve. Staying abstinent is in the best interest of my health and sanity. Each day I ask for the courage to persevere. I know I need to do the footwork by shopping and preparing the proper foods. I also pray to be willing to surrender my will to my Higher Power's care. I pray for the courage to remain humble.

For today, I rejoice in knowing that each day of recovery gives me a clearer picture of how good life can be.

A Renewable Gift

On occasion, we resent the routine shopping and cooking that abstinent meals require. When this occurs, we can take a moment to remember that abstinence is a gift that is ours to cherish and to celebrate.

On those days when we are not enjoying abstinence, we need to examine our attitudes and perceptions. We can remind ourselves of what a blessing it is to have money to buy the food that we need. We can remind ourselves that because we are in good health, we are able to cook for ourselves.

The effort expended in examining our thinking is well worth it for a life free of bingeing, purging, restricting, exercising compulsively, and obsessing about food.

Our old way of living reaped only chaos and destruction. Because we were in our disease, we were blocked from a higher awareness.

Today, thanks to abstinence, we are aware. Thanks to recovery, we can direct that awareness toward gratitude and celebration of the life we live today.

For today, I thank God for this glorious gift of abstinence.

Spiritual Fitness

Today by the grace of God, I am abstinent. However, my continued abstinence and recovery are contingent upon my spiritual condition. On this journey, I have had many spiritual awakenings, and each one has strengthened my recovery. I cannot afford to feel at any point that I have arrived spiritually and can rest on my laurels.

The spiritual lessons I am learning must be remembered, treasured, and practiced daily if they are to sustain me. I must continue to learn and grow in wisdom. Otherwise, the old thought patterns – the negativity, fear, doubt, and focus on food – will return.

As living, dynamic creatures, we are never stagnant. We are always moving either forward or backward. As an addict, I cannot afford to backslide. I need not rush forward, either. I need to cultivate my spirituality and let God lead me gently along the path of this journey.

For today, I pray to be spiritually fit, and remain open to receiving more of God's wisdom.

Supporting Our Fellowship

Every group ought to be fully self-supporting, declining outside contributions. (FAA Tradition Seven)

Tradition Seven puts the responsibility for supporting our group squarely on our shoulders. That makes it truly our group. No one can dictate to us. We are independent and self-supporting. We owe favors or special treatment to no one because we do not accept outside contributions.

What money we contribute at each meeting is up to our conscience. We keep in mind our group's expenses, including rent, literature, Intergroup, and a donation to World Service. We know how to work together within our guidelines to raise funds when the treasury is low.

We may occasionally think about how much easier it would be to accept outside donations. However, we realize that being self-supporting is a source of spiritual strength and self-respect.

For today, I give back to FAA what I have received.

I Am Never Alone

Before finding FAA, I felt alone. I couldn't believe anyone else could relate to the insanity of my disease. I couldn't imagine that anyone else ate food from the trash, consumed boxes of cookies, or stole candy from their children.

Now that I'm in recovery, I know that I am never alone. My Higher Power is always there for me, ready to show me His will, and ready to relieve me of my diseased thinking. By picking up the phone or going on the computer, I can connect to other food addicts who are just like me. Even when I feel justified and experience a dire need to pick up sugar, flour, or wheat, I just have to hold on for one more minute, one more hour, one more day. God always puts the right people in my life.

Like any other skill, the art of living one day at a time must be practiced. When it comes right down to it, what was it that caused me so much anxiety two months ago? Or last week? I can't remember.

For today, I reach out to God and my fellow food addicts so that I'm never alone.

Surrender to Win

Surrender is a continual process. I did not accept surrender willingly. For years I tried to do it my way, until this disease truly beat me. FAA was the last game in town. And I couldn't do another round in the ring with this addiction.

However, because I was beaten I became teachable. Through humility, I was given the strength to follow others, to ask for help, and to report my food to a sponsor. Eating addictive food was no longer an option. Each surrender leads to more surrender, such as simplifying my food, letting go of my trigger foods, and rotating my food.

Surrender also comes into other areas of my life. I can see today that I am powerless over people, places, and things, such as my family, my coworkers, and my boss. This recognition means that I am applying the wisdom gained in my recovery to the fullest.

For today, I am mindful that God is in the driver's seat.

Feelings, not Facts

Pride and jealousy are character defects that many of us share. For instance, we may feel that everyone has it better than us. This is not the truth, but a feeling. We have at times acted out on these feelings, because we confused them with facts. Our pride and isolation kept us stuck until we hurt enough to look inside and turn to our Higher Power for the real facts.

When we do our Fourth Step, we may find that our selfish desires and insatiable appetite have kept us blind to the truth. As we continue to work the Steps, we find in Steps Eight and Nine that we have to make some heartfelt amends for our insensitive behavior. We are willing to do so in order to heal from within. This is when we grow by leaps and bounds.

For today, I admit my character defects and do not confuse feelings with facts.

My Higher Power's Plan for Me

Help me learn that food is to nourish my body so my spirit can carry out your plans for me. (FAA Seventh Step Prayer)

When I was eating addictive foods, I had a difficult time making a connection with my Higher Power. I'm sure that God was right where I had left God – it was me who had made it harder to hear what God had to say or to feel any gentle nudging.

Now that I abstain from sugar, flour, and wheat, it's much easier to make that daily connection with God. The amazing part is that not only does God point me in the right direction if I take the time to ask, but also God guides me on the journey to wherever God thinks is best for me.

Some days are harder than others, and those are the days that I ask God to take my hand. God has never left me in the lurch. Now that I am learning to choose the foods that will nourish my body and spirit, I get the chance to make amends to myself for all the years that I was in the disease and unable or unwilling to carry out God's plans.

For today, I use food to fuel my body and listen to God's plan for me.

A Package I Won't Return

As far as food and weight were concerned, I once believed that my options were limited. To maintain a slim weight, I would simply have to tolerate cravings and anxiety. My other choice was to accept excess weight in exchange for the comfort and pleasure of eating what I desired, which was, of course, refined carbohydrates.

I could not accept either package in its entirety, so I continually exchanged one for the other. When I grew weary of the excess weight, I'd diet and tolerate anxiety and cravings just to be thin. When those feelings grew unbearable, I'd again turn to addictive foods and accept the inevitable weight gain. It was back and forth endlessly.

With recovery I find, miraculously, that I can have it all. On a food plan free of refined carbohydrates, I maintain a healthy weight without endless cravings. With support from the fellowship and the emotional recovery that comes from working the Steps, I no longer experience the intense anxiety that living without sedating foods once produced.

Freedom from cravings, emotional stability, and a slender body – the serenity package! I never dreamed I could have so much. I never imagined that God could be so good.

For today, I thank God for abstinence, and I ask for the wisdom to dismiss any thoughts of returning the gift.

Set Your Sights on Recovery

For today, I surrender to Step One and admit that I am powerless over my food addiction. I pray to my Higher Power for the courage and for the commitment to follow the FAA food plan. I do not listen to my disease and try another feeble attempt to control. I resign from the debating team and focus on recovery.

With surrender to Step One, I acknowledge that I have a biochemical disease. I have a daily reprieve. As I answer the Step One questions, I do not beat myself up for what I did in the past. I can leave the past in the past, realizing that my actions were sincere attempts to be well. By admitting my powerlessness, I open many new doors filled with countless miracles.

With sugar, wheat, and flour out of my body today, I accept that I have this disease without shaming or blaming myself. With this understanding that I am who I am, I can now focus on the present.

For today, I regard food only as nourishment so that I can focus on using my gifts and talents for a higher purpose.

Unwelcome Visitors

Sugar, flour, and wheat are no longer welcome visitors in the temple of my body. In the past, whenever I allowed these visitors in, they conducted themselves disgracefully. The moment I opened the door to what I thought would be just one or two of these substances, many more came charging in, and they brought with them an endless procession of rowdy friends. They argued endlessly when I tried to usher them out. They promised to behave. But the instant that I would relent, they would resume their mischief. They wreaked havoc on my body and disrupted my plans. Worst of all, they came between my Higher Power and me.

When I started working the FAA program and became abstinent, I was able to shut the door firmly on sugar, flour, and wheat. Occasionally, these unwelcome visitors knock on my door. Sometimes I'm tempted to let them back in, just to silence their cries. Instead, I pray, and they always go away, leaving me in peace.

At first the quiet space in my temple felt like emptiness. The former chaos, although unpleasant, had grown familiar. But today I welcome serenity. My temple is filled with good company today – and lots of laughter, light, and joy.

For today, I thank God for restoring my temple to a serene and stately abode.

Moving Mountains

Nothing is impossible with God's help. God gives me the strength to move mountains (if it is God's will that the mountains be moved). God wants me to prosper and succeed in life and to carry an honorable reputation representing God's love and grace. God wants me to recover from food addiction, and I show God my love and gratitude by reaching out to others.

God gives me the strength and ability to move mountains, but I must pick up the shovel and move one pile of dirt at a time. Through trust, I cultivate love, joy, peace, patience, kindness, goodness, faithfulness, gentleness, and self-control.

Today I have a food plan and a blueprint for life. I have a disease and I have a solution for that disease. I am responsible for accepting the solution. When I am tempted to relapse, God always shows me a way out.

For today, I am aware of what I must do next to take responsibility for my life in recovery and to carry this message to those who suffer.

Embracing Our Differences

How many times have we longed to be normal in our response to food? It is easy to think of ourselves as being different from people outside of FAA because we weigh and measure our food. Because we abstain from sugar, flour, and wheat. Because we eat three abstinent meals and a metabolic with nothing in between. At first, some   of us view the food plan as punishment.

In recovery, however, we come to believe that abstinence is the highest form of self-love. We weigh and measure and take all of the other actions that are needed around food because we love ourselves.

We need to look at our food plan with gratitude. We are gaining something – something greater than we could ever have imagined.

Perhaps instead of seeing ourselves as different, we can begin to see ourselves as pioneers who are establishing a new and healthy way to relate to food. Who knows how many lives we can touch for the good? We can discard our old ideas of what is "normal" or of what is rewarding. After all, if we have an answer that can help many, many suffering people, isn't it okay to be different?

For today, I believe that being different means being sane and healthy.

Facing Life's Challenges

How can I handle situations in which I am confronted by sugar, flour, or wheat? Sometimes, it might be the desserts calling to me or some annoying person who keeps asking me if I want more food. When someone invites me to eat something I know is not on my plan, my disease screams, "Yes! I want it all." My recovery reminds me that my abstinence is the most important priority of my life.

So what can I do to meet these challenges? First, I follow this simple plan of recovery, starting with prayer to the God of my understanding asking for all the help I will need. Second, I cherish my abstinence and remember that I am responsible for remaining abstinent. I can read FAA literature, write about my feelings, and reach out to other loving food addicts. I can fill my life with activities that are fun. I can give myself the freedom to make my needs known and to get up and leave if it is clear to me that my needs will not be met. I can do all this kindly and quietly, assured that I do not need to break my abstinence.

The beauty of using the tools and following the program is that continued abstinence helps me work the Steps that will lead me closer to the God of my understanding.

For today, I ask my Higher Power to give me the strength to get through sticky situations.

Shelter From the Storm

There are days when thunder and lightning are never-ending. Just when I think the storm is over, the rain starts again. It's beyond my control. What is within my control is how I react to these conditions or how I help myself deal with the stormy weather. I have many healthy options.

FAA is my safe haven against all types of adversity. What I do know for sure is that maintaining my abstinence is my first line of defense. Without that, I am battered by the winds. I am confused. I am lost.

No matter how dark the skies are; no matter how hard the rain falls; no matter how scary the howling wind sounds; all of these things shall pass. There is bound to be a rainbow, and the sun will once again shine. When that happens, I will be thankful for the warmth it provides, and I will be thankful that together we were able to weather the storm.

For today, I can weather whatever problems I face with the help of FAA.

My Higher Power Guides Me

When we first look at Step Seven, it might not make sense that another Step is dealing with removal of our shortcomings – just another way to say character defects. Our sponsors are quick to point out we don't need to intellectualize the Steps; we just need to work them.

Each time one of our character defects rears its ugly head, we may feel humiliated and confused, but we learn that this is just part of the process.

With humility, we become teachable, and our wall of denial breaks down. Facing our character defects often brings embarrassment and discomfort.

Even though we feel that we are ready to have God remove our defects of character, they can still creep back into our lives. We once again experience the despair and pain that comes from acting on our own self-will. It is only when we stop trying to rid ourselves of our shortcomings and instead surrender them to a Higher Power that a beam of light guides us.

For today, I am grateful that the humiliation and the shortcomings of my past are no longer part of my present.

Lessons to Learn

Acknowledging that I am powerless over my food addiction has relieved me of the misery associated with feeble attempts to control the foods I put into my mouth. Instead of feeling self-pity and remorse in looking back over all the years of denial, I instead realize that these were the lessons I needed to learn to understand this devastating and deadly disease of food addiction.

Today I realize that my disease needed me to live in the muddy morass of negativity in order for it to flourish. What a gift from my Higher Power to be led into the rooms of Food Addicts Anonymous. With a clean body and a clear head, I have the ability to sort out what and who is in my best interest.

I am now free to live a useful and fulfilling life. Without sugar, flour, and wheat clogging up my body and brain, I allow myself to be open to all the wonderful miracles of life.

For today, I ask my Higher Power to help me remain teachable and abstinent.

Laughing at Our Rationalizations

Most of us in FAA realize that our lives have been saved, extended or enhanced by becoming abstinent. Many of us attribute the enhanced quality of our lives to this program. With an appreciation and acknowledgement that is so deep, profound, and significant, we may begin to think that we always have to be in a serious frame of mind. But commitment and seriousness need not exclude humor.

We can often find humor in our diseased thinking of the past. For example, our cloudy thinking may have told us that turbinado sugar is not sugar. What part of the word S-U-G-A-R did we not understand? Perhaps when we were measuring our food we used a steamroller to stuff as many vegetables as possible into a cup. Or we ate half of a watermelon because we said, "Isn't it the same as a cantaloupe?"

We can use humor to dismiss our irrational thoughts. We can use humor to help us let go of the past. We can let ourselves laugh at ourselves rather than beat ourselves up for the strange thoughts that we have in this disease.

For today, I ask my Higher Power to heal me with laughter.

A Clear Path

Being in the disease of food addiction is like living in an overgrown garden. Weeds choke every crevice. Flowers are neglected and starving for nourishment and love.

When our bodies are filled with sugar, flour and wheat, our minds are filled with the clutter of obsession, compulsion, and cravings. Guilt and remorse choke our thoughts. Our minds are too filled with negativity to connect with our Higher Power.

Each day that we are abstinent and working the Steps, our bodies get the nourishment they need, and our minds are given room to grow. We feel better about ourselves, and we handle life's ups and downs with more grace.

Abstinence allows us to clear the gloom and clutter from our minds and lives and to let the sun shine on the path before us. The garden in our mind is weeded, so that it can bloom with love, life, and joy.

For today, as I use my recovery tools, I thank God that my path is getting clearer.

A Healthy Environment

We need our fellow food addicts. Alone, we may quickly succumb to unhealthy influences.

Movies, television, and magazines sometimes portray being underweight as far more desirable than being a healthy weight. FAA provides a solution with which to counter that madness. We are routinely assured that dieting is not appropriate for food addicts; that a healthy weight is a good weight, and that fashion trends are irrelevant to our recovery.

Our fellowship supports many values contrary to the mainstream: taking time for ourselves rather than overworking; developing our spiritual life rather than developing our wallets; and giving service without expecting a reward.

We strengthen these values within ourselves by participating in a fellowship that practices these principles in all its affairs. Without our meetings, we are in danger of returning to the foods that have become commonplace in our society – sugar, flour, and wheat.

In FAA, we are grateful that we have redefined healthy eating and living.

For today, I am grateful for the FAA fellowship that supports my recovery.

Going to Any Lengths

"Being willing to go to any lengths" is one of those catch phrases that we may hear again and again in the FAA rooms. We may ask ourselves what *going to any lengths* means to us as individuals. If an FAA meeting is 10 miles away, does *going to any lengths* mean attending that meeting, even if it's inconvenient? How about if the meeting is 25 miles away? 50? 100? 200? Where do we cross the line between *going to any lengths* and doing something that's self-punishing?

Perhaps the phrase *going to any lengths* is relative to each of us. Only I can know my own personal meaning of *going to any lengths* as it pertains to growing in my recovery, just as only I can know if I am abstinent. The answers lie in my heart, which is where I find my Higher Power.

I ask God to help me listen to my heart and distinguish God's voice from the voice of the disease. I ask to be connected to myself and to others. The disease takes me away from myself. God brings me back.

For today, I ask for the wisdom to know what lengths I need to go to to follow God's will for me.

Choose to Cooperate

"A Higher Power is necessary to our recovery, but is not solely sufficient. We must also cooperate with this Higher Power and work for our recovery." (<u>Food Addicts Anonymous</u>, *Some Thoughts on Spirituality*)

Before finding recovery, my addictive substances, especially sugar, flour, and wheat, were my higher power. They were what I called on to soothe me, to celebrate with, and to console me. I think of them now as a kind of *lower* power. The substances that I relied on to keep me sane, instead, kept me feeling out of control.

I tried for years to manipulate, control, and limit the use of my addictive substances, all the while getting sicker and sicker. Still, I turned to these substances again and again, always expecting a different outcome.

Today, through a loving Higher Power and FAA, I have found a better way. I do what I believe to be the will of my Higher Power by remaining abstinent. Nothing can take away this recovery. I now have the power of choice in what I eat. I am maturing and taking responsibility for my actions. I recognize that I have a biochemical disease that can be arrested by abstaining from all of my triggers.

For today, I choose to work with my Higher Power and seek wellness, love, and an abstinent life.

Choosing What We Say

Today we refrain from vocalizing every thought or feeling that we have. With God's guidance, we communicate in the language of recovery. When moved to speak, we first ask ourselves, "Is it thoughtful? Is it helpful? Is it kind? Is it honest?" Only then do we say what we want to say.

If we are tempted to talk negatively about others or about ourselves, we ask our Higher Power for help. We learn to be silent until the negative thoughts subside. We do not need to speak our negative thoughts and feelings out loud.

In recovery we pray that we can distinguish between fleeting destructive thoughts and thoughts that are positive and caring. Freedom from impulsive and indiscriminate expression is a wonderful gift of recovery.

For today, I humbly ask God to remove my shortcomings and guide me in expressing my thoughts.

Trust the Plan

There are times when someone asks me, "Why can't you have this particular food? It doesn't have sugar in it. It only contains honey. Why can't you have it?"

How do I explain to a non-food addict that I am addicted to sugars? How do I explain that sugar is not just in the obvious places? It goes by many different names. It hides in less obvious seemingly innocent foods, such as some dairy products, certain frozen meats, and canned fruits and vegetables. A valuable tool to help guide us with these choices is the FAA literature that lists the names of sugars.

When someone starts questioning me however, I start to wonder, is it possible that just a little bit of sugar won't affect me? But I've done the research. I have fought for years to have just a little bit of something. It never happened. So why take the chance? And why question? Being smart got me into the unmanageable mess I was in when I first came to FAA. The food plan makes perfect sense for my body, and that is good enough for me.

For today, I stay with what works and remember from where I came.

Facing the Fear

Fear is deeply ingrained in my being. It is who I had become as a result of a lot of circumstances. Fear held its place in my life to protect me from harm before I learned how to trust and depend on my Higher Power.

Before recovery, I didn't trust anyone and didn't expect anyone to help me. After experiencing a better life through abstinence and a faithful dependence on the Twelve Step process, I realized that my Higher Power didn't give me a spirit of fear, but of love, power, and a sound mind. It was my choice whether to react in fear or in faith.

Today, I am happy, free from food obsession or addictions, and free from the need to be perfect and right and in control. I am okay. I have enough, I do enough, and I am enough. I have courage and I am empowered by the God of my understanding to step out of my comfort zone. I may be afraid, but fear doesn't make me crumble and die. I am better each time I live to testify about the goodness and love that I have found.

As a result of working the Twelve Steps in my life, faith has replaced my fear.

For today, I face the fear and do it anyway with my Higher Power's help.

Unconditional Abstinence

Today I accept and surrender to unconditional abstinence. Turning to the food is not an option for me. I will not even entertain the thought.

When we say "No!" to our children and mean it, they eventually come to accept what we say and move on. But when we waiver, we open the door to a deluge of "why not's?" We have no peace, nor do they.

So it is with this disease. If I waiver and entertain even the remotest option of picking up my addictive substance, I struggle through the day. The addict within me will argue, pester, and continually seek to persuade. I may wonder why I am not experiencing the serenity of recovery. It is because neither I nor the addict within me is satisfied. It is uncomfortable sitting on the fence!

When that little voice within demands instant comfort and gratification from addictive foods, I can gently but firmly respond, "No, not today."

For today, I ask my Higher Power for the strength to treat my abstinence and myself with the respect we deserve.

My Swim Coach

Learning to swim in deep water can be a terrifying experience. But if we are lucky, we have a loving teacher who teaches us to just relax and float. We are amazed when we find that we are safe.

In much the same way, our sponsors teach us how to float and how to swim. We just need to listen, trust, and then do what we are asked to do.

We can become willing to let go of the fears of our past. We are free to live in serenity and joy. It begins when we are willing to take direction.

For today, I trust those who have walked the road of recovery and who call me forward to walk with them.

Change in Attitude

Made a list of all persons we had harmed and became willing to make amends to them all. (FAA Step Eight)

So much of my progress toward serenity in FAA depends on a change in my attitude. Step Eight asks us to become willing. After we have been progressively led through the first seven Steps to change our attitude about our Higher Power and ourselves, we turn our attention to others.

With self-forgiveness we realize that defects of character have caused us harm in all our relationships. How lucky that we are directed to make amends after we have humbly asked in the Seventh Step to have those shortcomings removed. Step Eight cannot happen until we are thoroughly honest in the first seven Steps. Until we give up our negative, destructive attitudes, we cannot mend our actions toward others or ourselves.

When we put our trust in God, it is easier to accept others as they are and refrain from making judgments. When we are not in a position of judging, we can be more inclined to be understanding and recognize our part in mending relationships.

This Step does not ask us to take action. All we need to do is change our attitude and be willing to make amends.

For today, I ask for the willingness to make my amends with love and gratitude.

Spiritual Lessons

All things happen for a reason. Although it may not be readily apparent, all situations offer a spiritual lesson.

As I continue to live an abstinent life, I recognize these lessons more easily. My recovery teaches me to take good care of myself. My disagreement with another teaches me that my views may be too rigid. Whenever things don't go my way, I have the opportunity to practice patience, perseverance, trust in God, and surrender all that I cannot control. When I look for my part in every situation, I see lessons to be learned.

For today, I ask God to help me to recognize and appreciate the spiritual lessons presented to me daily.

We Want to Have Fun

Somewhere in our disease, we figured that fun wasn't for us. We somehow figured we weren't deserving of it, nor did we have the energy to follow through with fun plans when we did make them.

In recovery, we are reclaiming our childlike wonder and relearning how to have fun without focusing on the food. Our urge to have fun is being cultivated. We can see that laughter improves our mental health.

We can start having fun by calling a program friend and making a play date. It needn't be too far out of our comfort zone. Just a little at a time. Once we have experienced some successful play dates, we can expand our playgroup. We can invite more friends and plan a day trip.

The momentum of planning for playtime will begin to carry us, and the fun times will expand. The secret is to stay in recovery and use the recovery tools.

How did we live so long without having fun?

For today, I experience joy, fun, and laughter, whether I am alone or with others and enjoy the energy that laughter brings.

Keeping Myself Safe

If a child said to me, "I'd like to play ball in the middle of the street," I'd be quick to tell him no. If he were particularly determined, I might take other measures to ensure his safety. I might lock the door until his desire passed.

In recovery, I am as vigilant with myself as I would be with a child. I say no to desires that will hurt me. I stay abstinent so that I can be clear-headed and able to discern what will and will not hurt me. I take precautions to ensure my own safety. I know that amid the loud rumblings of the disease, my belief system might be distorted. I am patient with myself. I do whatever it takes to remain abstinent, trusting that I am getting better with each abstinent moment.

I might not always know what is best for me. That is why it is important for me to stay close to the program and to people who will lovingly help me make healthy choices and to change what needs changing.

For today, I ask God to help me be willing to make changes. I ask God to help me love myself as much as I love others.

Desiring Recovery

We learn in FAA that food addiction is a disease of the body, mind, and spirit. When sugar, flour, and wheat are cruising through our system, we cannot fight the physical cravings to get more food. Nor can we fight our own thinking, which may include wishing that we had a desire to live.

Sometimes all we can do is ask God for the willingness to desire recovery, so that we may discover our peace and contentment.

A food addict's mind cannot think its way abstinent. If we have never known normalcy, how could we possibly even know what to ask for? We probably knew *high* and no doubt we knew *low*, but we never really knew what peace felt like.

If we are open, we can get a hint of what peace is from our fellow food addicts who are a little further down the path of abstinence and recovery. This helps us move forward in desiring our own recovery.

For today, I ask God to give me the desire to seek recovery.

Attitude of Gratitude

Today I am grateful first to wake up and to show my gratitude. I will prepare an abstinent breakfast. Before I eat, I will give thanks to my Higher Power for all that is in front of me. I know that by eating an abstinent breakfast I am doing the proper thing for my mind and body. I know that what is in front of me will be enough to sustain me until lunch.

I will give thanks before I eat my abstinent lunch that I will be satisfied in body, mind, and spirit to be carried until dinner, when I will again give thanks before I eat that my body and mind will be satisfied until my metabolic adjustment.

After my metabolic adjustment I will again give thanks to my Higher Power for being by my side and carrying me abstinently through the day.

For today, I trust that as long as I do the footwork in recovery, my Higher Power will take care of all the situations and people in my life.

Turning it Over

Working the Steps results in many changes in our outlook and in our behavior. As we work the Steps and stay abstinent on a daily basis, the cravings for food are lifted. Our shortcomings begin to be removed. Our Higher Power does for us what we cannot do for ourselves.

For years I tried to overpower or ignore my cravings. Despite dieting, fasting, bingeing, and purging, the cravings continued. I made resolutions and promises. "I won't be late any more." "I'll stick to my diet." "I won't gossip." But the character defects continued.

With abstinence and working the Steps, I am relieved of the cravings. I turn my defects over to my Higher Power on a daily basis. Now I know that I don't have to do this alone.

For today, I choose to turn my life and my will over to a Power greater than myself.

Prepare to Seek Forgiveness

Made a list of persons we had harmed and became willing to make amends to them all. (FAA Step Eight)

In active addiction, we wreaked plenty of havoc. We consumed more than our share of household food, frustrating those with whom we lived. We lied in order to hide, defend, and continue with our addictive eating. We stole food when necessary.

We squandered money on binge foods, weight loss schemes, or on clothing in so many different sizes. We were emotionally and sometimes physically unavailable to those we loved. We were hurtful because of our unpredictable and irrational behavior.

We neglected friendships and were irresponsible or unreliable employees. Moreover, we relentlessly abused and neglected our body, mind, and spirit.

In Step Eight, we review and acknowledge the harm and suffering inflicted during our years of active addiction. We develop an even deeper appreciation and gratitude for our recovery, which has delivered us from our old way of life. Step Eight prepares us for making amends in Step Nine and for making a commitment to leave the past behind.

For today, I ask that God be with me as I calmly and clearly review the destructive nature of my life and prepare to make amends.

Recovery Enhances Vacation

I used to work, work, work until the pressure overwhelmed me. A binge served as a release valve. Once reengaged in life, I would again overwork and overdo, and the cycle repeated. The food served as the sole escape from my relentless inner drive. I never experienced healthy, recuperative rest.

Today I enjoy my time off. It is not imposed as the result of a binge, nor is it an opportunity to binge. I no longer sacrifice my free time to this disease. Free time is now an opportunity to do the things I love – to be truly present with my friends and family, to pursue creative activities, to enjoy outings, and to participate fully in life.

Healthy, recuperative rest is a joy, a blessing, and essential to my recovery. I plan for it, I am entitled to it, and I take it. If I do not slow myself down, the food will likely trip me up.

For today, I pray that I may live a moderately paced life and that I balance work with rest, fun, and family and friends.

Letting My Gratitude Shine

As I reflect on the gifts given to me through FAA, am I grateful? Many times gratitude is another aspect of my recovery that needs to be taken out of the closet every now and then and looked at. Like a precious gem or anything of rare beauty, knowing it is tucked away in a safe place may give me a sense of security, but holding it out in the light is the way to truly appreciate it.

There are many ways I can take my gratitude out of the shadows and let the light of appreciation shine. I can reach out to newcomers. I can call someone in the program who has been struggling. I can take on a service commitment. The list is endless. Saying I have gratitude is never the same as putting my gratitude into action.

There are many ways of giving back. There are many ways of allowing my gratitude to shimmer and shine. Gratitude always looks best out there in the light for all to see. When I give back, it sparkles best.

For today, I will put my gratitude into action.

Healthy Risk Taking

Perfectionism was my attempt at control. Paradoxically, the perfectionism controlled me. Either I had to be tops in whatever I did or I didn't do it. Obviously, there were many times I did very little. My fear immobilized me. I would sit on the sidelines and watch others. I became a spectator in this thing we call life.

One of the great truths of life is that we all learn from our mistakes. If I don't attempt something, I prevent myself from the opportunity of learning.

In my abstinence, I am learning to take chances. It is important for my own abstinence to reach out to others with my concerns and fears. It may be scary to allow myself to be vulnerable, but if I walk through these fears, I always come out better on the other side.

For today, I benefit from taking some healthy risks, knowing I cannot control the outcome.

I Am Not My Body

Today I look at my body as a creation of my Higher Power and believe that my Higher Power doesn't make junk. I nurture the wonderful machine that I am. This is another way to say thank you to my Higher Power for bringing me to FAA, for never giving up on me, and for loving me when I could not love myself.

I no longer need to get weighed daily on the scale because I weigh my food on the scale. I accept my body just as it is and I am thankful for all that it does for me. I see what is good, what is beautiful. I do not judge. My body houses my spirit, and I am in touch with my spirit today.

For today, I look at my body as a gift from my Higher Power, perfect in all its imperfections.

Full Measures

Either I want recovery or I don't. And I want to recover.

If I want recovery, I am willing to take the Steps and work this program with every fiber of my being. I am willing to surrender my will and commit to doing the next right thing – one day at a time. I am willing to follow the directions no matter what. It's a matter of life and death. I am willing to do whatever it takes to keep my abstinence.

I am grateful to know that I am not doing this alone. I pray for fellow FAA members as they pray for me. I take the Steps with a full measure of honesty in order to receive a full measure of abstinence.

I honor my fellow members and my sponsor by giving back what is so freely given to me. In giving back, I get another 24 hours of abstinence.

For today, I believe that half measures equal half a life, for which I will not settle.

Willing to Recover

I have to be willing to go to any lengths to recover. This means that I have to do things that I may not feel like doing. If I want to recover, I have to do the footwork. I have to weigh and measure my food, report it to my sponsor, and then eat what I have committed. I make sure I have the food that I need and not depend on others to have what I need. I plan to succeed.

I know that meeting-makers make it, so I go to meetings. I read recovery literature and work the Steps. I live my recovery, not just talk the talk.

I stay humble and teachable. I share what I have with others in recovery. I stay connected with my Higher Power, keeping myself spiritually fit.

Recovery requires work. Relapse takes no effort at all. If I keep doing what I need to do, I will stay in recovery.

For today, I gratefully go to any lengths and put my recovery before all else in my life.

Hope Lives in the FAA Rooms

When we were in our disease, we may have looked happy and successful. However, when we come to FAA we were able to show our true feelings, which we had buried.

The first couple of years in recovery are sometimes especially hard. We may experience depression and pain due to distorted thinking and false conceptions. Keeping it simple, going to meetings, talking frequently to a sponsor, and working the Steps help. Giving service, no matter how small, keeps our memories green. Sharing with our sponsor and sponsoring others brings new light to our inner self.

When we persevere, we eventually find serenity and a way of life unlike any we've ever dared to hope for or felt we deserved. We experience peace, clear thinking, manageable emotions, and a trusting spirit. We make new and healthier relationships, because we are more honest and open. Our relationships with family members improve as well, thanks to our Higher Power's healing and the FAA principles.

We will know a new freedom, and our outsides will match our insides.

For today, I show my happiness and gratitude by sharing my recovery with another food addict.

Making a List

Made a list of all persons we had harmed, and became willing to make amends to them all. (FAA Step Eight)

In Step Eight we are getting ready to make amends for the harm we have done, thus it is an appropriate time to meditate on forgiveness. I start by forgiving those who have harmed me. I am then able to move more willingly into asking forgiveness of those I have harmed.

If I have a feeling of guilt about someone, I meditate with the spirit of humility and add that person's name to my list. I don't take refuge in feelings of defensiveness by telling myself, "I only said or did what I did because she said so and so." I focus only on any inappropriate action that I took.

I put my name prominently on the list of people to whom I need to make amends. I may have ignored my own needs for years. I resolve to change all that. I will take time to get a medical checkup, rest, and play. I give myself the love and consideration I accord others.

I dwell on my Higher Power's love for me, which helps me then extend that love to family, friends, and even strangers on the street.

For today, I ask my Higher Power for willingness to make the amends that will help rebuild my life.

The Monster is Gone

I used to think that the disease of food addiction involved only addictive foods, but there is so much more. The disease snakes around my brain, telling me that bad is good, right is wrong, sick is healthy. In the beginning of recovery, I could not trust anything that those voices in my head were telling me, because I was mired in disease. I had to depend on my sponsor and on other recovering FAA members to tell me what was good for me and what was not.

I have come to understand that as I remain abstinent, the disease gets chipped away, and my true self remains. So what I need, want, and desire has always been with me. I just need to shed the layers of disease that block it. I do this by exposing the lies that the disease tells me. I acknowledge the lie, write it down, tell my sponsor, and then turn it over to my Higher Power.

Doors open up to me as I remain in recovery. I start to experience new ways of doing, thinking, and feeling. It's as if I get a second chance to grow up. As I share my truth, my light shines more brightly. Sharing my truth helps others share theirs.

For today, I cherish the second chance I am given through abstinence.

Humility Keeps Me Teachable

Humility allows me to accept that I am a food addict. I have come to see that my addiction to sugar, flour, and wheat is at the root of every problem in my life. Humility is not in my vocabulary after I pick up addictive foods. Self-will and insane thinking patterns take over as my body chemistry changes. These changes tax my brain and bodily functions to the point that God can't get through to me. I am no longer talking. The sugar, flour, and wheat are.

I endeavor to practice humility in all my affairs each day and allow God to get through to me.

Humility comes in realizing that this disease cannot be fought by willpower alone or by me alone. I need the strength and support of a Higher Power and of the FAA group.

Humility comes in believing that my body knows and that my mind cannot control this disease. I become humble when I no longer try to justify my food needs to others.

As I grow spiritually and emotionally in FAA, my dealings with others become more honest and loving.

For today, I thank FAA for giving me a sense of humility and sincerity.

The Meaning of Acceptance

Acceptance is the key to my recovery.

Food addiction is a life-stealing disease. Although sugar, flour, and wheat may not kill me as quickly as a drug overdose, it will kill me over time. When I am in the disease of food addiction, I am part of the walking dead.

Acceptance is the first thing I must do, and I must do so with rigorous honesty. Without taking this step, I am merely play-acting, and my recovery ends when the play does.

Acceptance means freedom because it allows me to turn my troubles over to a power greater than myself for guidance. This greater power may include FAA, my sponsor, the literature, or phone calls to healthy friends.

Acceptance means direction. I am given clear direction in the mental, physical, and spiritual realms because I have the guidelines of this program to follow.

Acceptance means loving myself. I no longer have to hide in a food fog. Instead, the problems that I face become opportunities for spiritual growth.

For today, I accept, respect and love myself as I go through difficult situations.

The Gifts I Have Received in FAA

When I decided that I wanted what FAA had to offer, I followed the prescribed plan exactly. I stopped playing around. As a result, I received many gifts.

The gift of progress: Every time I relapsed, I learned something new, which helped get me to where I am now.

The gift of clarity: My head is clear to make better decisions.

The gift of freedom from cravings: Life is so much easier when I'm not in a constant battle.

The gift of relationships: A closer relationship with my Higher Power. All relationships are cleaner, more honest, and more open.

The gift of letting go: During stressful times, I feel a great sense of peace and believe that everything will turn out wonderfully, even without me worrying or trying to control it.

The gift of support: The support I get from fellow FAA members is amazing.

For today, I acknowledge and express my gratitude for all the gifts I have received.

Grateful for Freedom

I never gave much thought to freedom before FAA. My life held so many dark moments. There seemed to be real reasons for my resentment, anger and self-pity. After all, I had failed at many diets and continued to gain weight.

If it wasn't for meetings where we listen to other food addicts recount how the drive to eat addictive foods controls our lives, we might forget what addictive foods do to us – the prison of living in hopelessness and helplessness.

Even though members talked a lot about abstaining one day at a time, I knew it meant forever. After about ninety days, I still felt no sign of freedom. My sponsor would tell me to abstain from those foods I was craving just for today adding that after the physical cravings were gone the mental obsession hangs around.

After many years of abstinence, I'm finally grateful for the freedom FAA gives me. I learned I had a biochemical disease. It wasn't that I lacked willpower. By applying the Twelve Steps to my life, I can be free from the chains of resentment, anger and self-pity. The program promises I can live a free, useful, and happy life.

For today, I will be grateful for the freedom abstinence brings.

Slowing Down and Nourishing My Body

Before FAA, I never could enjoy a meal. I would eat rapidly, often alone, like a thief, as if I were doing something illegal. Chewing food and then spitting it out, insanely rationalizing that I wasn't really eating it; or taking small bites of food and then throwing out the rest, so I was never sure how much I was actually eating. I was eating for the buzz, and to numb my feelings.

Today I sit down at the table and enjoy my meals guilt-free because I know I am nourishing myself and I have every right to eat the food in front of me. I can eat slowly and savor my food. I like the different textures of my food, like the crunchiness of raw vegetables. I like the smell and taste of my food. I no longer need to douse my food with salt and sweeteners.

I believe that God has made the sensory aspects of eating pleasurable because eating is necessary for survival. I pray before my meals because my body is sacred, and taking care of it is a sacred act. I remind myself while eating that food is no longer my higher power.

For today, I maintain conscious contact with my Higher Power through conscious eating practices.

I Am a Miracle

When we stay around the rooms of FAA long enough, we become one of the miracles. I am a walking miracle today because of FAA.

Before program, I could not get from lunch to dinner without putting something in my mouth. It was both an unconscious and, at the same time, a deliberate action. I chewed gum until the sugar was gone and then replaced it with more. I drank diet sodas and had a constant dialogue going on in my head about food: what I should eat, what I wish I could eat, what I wish I had not eaten. I was ruled by the insanity of the disease.

No matter what my resolve was at the beginning of my day, it would soon melt. I was powerless over this addiction, and my unsuccessful attempts at control were actually out of my control. I felt hopeless and helpless. Then I found FAA.

Today I eat three weighed and measured meals plus a weighed and measured metabolic adjustment. I have no cravings, and I have a Higher Power in my life.

For today, I stay in the FAA rooms to watch miracles happen.

Higher Power Speaks Through Intuition

I am grateful that the FAA promises are starting to come true for me, because I am doing what I need to do. I am done trying to do things my way. I am done fooling around with the food plan to suit my needs.

I have begun to cherish my abstinence as never before. It is as though a switch has been flipped, and my thinking has become clear. I especially appreciate feeling that I can trust my intuition. I have come to believe that my intuition is a way in which my Higher Power speaks to me.

Clean abstinence has taken away the cravings and fogginess that took over my brain when I was in the food. I am able to maintain conscious contact with my Higher Power.

These are the Promises that I had never thought possible before abstinence and recovery. As I see them coming true for me, I can believe in long-term recovery. I can also share with my fellow food addicts that there is hope for recovery from food addiction.

For today, I share the Promises with others, encouraging them to stay for the miracles.

Sliver, Slice, Slab, Slob

The disease of food addiction never goes away. Our addictive minds can rationalize that one extra sliver of food that is on our food plan won't have any negative consequences.

Perhaps for a short time the damage of one sliver doesn't appear to us. We may not notice the slight loss of serenity. But a sliver inevitably leads to an extra slice as rampant self-will sets in. Even then, things may still appear to be fine. But extra slices add up to slabs. And slabs lead us back into the disease and tear us away from serenity. We begin feeling like slobs, even if we are abstaining from addictive foods.

Indulging in extra volume may be the first step in heading back down the path of sugar, flour, or wheat. The trick is to recognize that first sliver as dangerous, ask for help from our Higher Power and from our FAA friends, and avoid the rationalization that one bite, one sliver, won't make a difference.

One extra bite always does and always will make a difference, because we are food addicts.

For today, I ask my Higher Power for help in making sure I eat what I committed with no extra bites.

Came for Vanity, Stayed for Sanity

Let's admit it. Most of us came to FAA hoping it was a weight loss program and/or to make our bodies more attractive. The majority of us were overweight, some of us so severely obese that our lives were threatened. Some of us were so thin we knew we had to do something to look normal. No matter which end of the physical spectrum we were in when we came to FAA, our vanity brought us here more often than not.

As we became abstinent and our bodies became more of what we wanted, we realized that our lives had improved in many ways we had not anticipated. Many of us experienced a peace in our lives we had never had. We were relieved of food cravings and prideful thoughts that had plagued us. We became more intuitive, more centered, and our lives were more productive. For many, years of depression were lifted and a joy and delight in our lives sprung from our souls.

We were saner than ever. The vanity we once desired was replaced with a sanity we had never known. This sanity allows us to remain abstinent.

For today, I ask my Higher Power to give me the willingness to recognize and appreciate the sanity coming into my life.

A Perfect Union

Abstinence is like a good marriage. I may not always feel absolutely loving toward my abstinence, but I know that we are right for each other, and I know that I want the relationship to last. It's wonderful to have the peace and security as the direct result of that understanding.

Honoring my commitment to abstinence means that I decline the temptation of a tryst with chocolate, a side-fling with sugar, or an affair with flour. I cannot have it both ways. I cannot have a stable, happy recovery life and dabble with my former lovers, too. There is a reason that I left them all in the first place – they abused me terribly.

I don't take my commitment to abstinence lightly. I take measures daily to ensure that my decisions around food and relationships with others will be what my Higher Power wants for me. I make choices that will keep me sane and honest. It is good to have a choice today. I choose abstinence. It always treats me right!

For today, I thank my Higher Power for blessing me with a healthy and happy relationship with food.

Writing

Writing is a quiet, powerful tool of our Twelve-Step fellowship. Writing helps us reach deep inside ourselves and discover the good and the not-so-good that makes us who and what we are. It gives us a foundation for our progress in recovery.

Sometimes our writings may find a common theme: "I don't feel good." We may begin to pity ourselves because we feel this way. We learn in taking our own inventory that we are to practice the opposite of our defects. If we feel self-pity, we can take action. Our Higher Power will show us what action we need to take in any given moment. It may be reading, writing, praying the Serenity Prayer, or talking. Using the tools will help us get to the root of a problem so that we can find a solution.

For today, I use whatever tools are necessary to help me out of the hole of disease. I pray for the willingness to do whatever is necessary to help me feel connected again.

Relying on Experience, Strength and Hope

FAA should remain forever nonprofessional, but our service centers may employ special workers. (FAA Tradition Eight)

Carrying the message to others is a necessary part of working the Twelve Steps. Food addicts helping food addicts. We give freely what we have been given. If we were paid for this spiritual work, the words might not have the same meaning. Counselors, therapists, nutritionists, and doctors can play an important role; however, this must always be separate from the recovery sought and found through the fellowship of FAA. Varied professionals offer varied treatments. FAA does not. We have one message.

Many professionals within the fellowship attend FAA meetings for their own recovery. They are never recognized for their credentials at meetings. They simply share their experiences as FAA members.

Tradition Eight makes provision for some paid workers in our World Service Office. Our fellowship needs skilled workers to perform the tasks necessary for communication with groups, to facilitate the printing and distribution of literature, maintain the FAA website and to be sure we operate in compliance with state and federal laws.

For today, I ask God to help me remember that I am just another member of FAA.

Finding Forgiveness

Forgiveness promotes feelings of compassion, optimism, and hope. When I first came to FAA, I was holding on to so much hurt from past relationships that I didn't think forgiveness was something I wanted in my life. I didn't want to let go of the hurt; I wanted revenge. In working the Steps, I have found that lack of forgiveness was the biggest obstacle to my willingness to make amends to those I had harmed. As long as I was focusing on what they did wrong, I wasn't able to see my part in the situation and make amends for the harm I caused. Even if my part is only 5% of the problem, it is that 5% that can propel me back into eating addictive foods.

I have learned that there are things I can do to forgive those who have hurt me. I can write about the reasons I am angry or hurt and share it with my sponsor. I can pray that the person will receive all the good gifts in life that I want for myself. I can pray for the spirit of forgiveness. I can then begin to see forgiveness as an action that allows me to recover.

When I take steps toward forgiving, the willingness to make amends comes. I become willing not just to apologize, but also to truly change my actions.

For today, I ask my Higher Power for a spirit of forgiveness and the willingness to make amends.

First Things First

Made a list of all persons we had harmed and became willing to make amends to them all. (FAA Step Eight)

Making amends involves some kind of regret. Many of us food addicts aren't very good with apologies. With the help of our sponsor, though, we may find that we've been putting the cart before the horse. Step Eight says to make a list of all the people we had harmed and then become willing to make amends.

We may find it hard to think not in terms of who hurt us but, rather, who we have hurt. We may be used to taking on the role of the victim. It helps to listen to other recovering food addicts talk about their willingness.

Our sponsor may suggest that we put ourselves at the top of the list of people we have harmed. It may be painful to look at the part we've played in our own demise. But we can take comfort in knowing that there is no deadline for doing Step Eight. By listening to others, we can keep it simple and trust our Higher Power to show us who, what, when, and where we need to make amends. The next step is to amend the wrong by not repeating the harm. And then we are changed – for the better.

For today, I thank my Higher Power that my amends are an ongoing process fueled by love.

A Food Addict's D.T.'s

We in FAA have our own D.T.'s – Disease Talking. Our disease is cunning and powerful and may lead us away from serenity and abstinence and down a very dark path.

The D.T.'s may first be recognized when we start trivializing the actions we must take – or not take – in order to recover from food addiction. For instance, our disease might tell us, "It won't really matter if I put this extra little bite in my mouth" or "So what if I don't weigh and measure today. I'll do it tomorrow." At times our disease may whisper, "Don't bother calling your sponsor today" or "Don't make that amends" or "Don't waste time praying today."

Our thoughts and actions matter and we must expose the voice of disease whenever we hear it. Our disease tries to lull us into thinking that we have some control over our addiction. It tries to get us to believe that it is OK to take back just a little of our own will.

Many of us have found that listening to our disease puts us into relapse. So we turn over our D.T.'s to our Higher Power and ask for help. We can adopt another meaning for DT: Direction Taking (from our Higher Power).

For today, I ask my Higher Power to give me the wisdom to recognize my diseased thoughts and be willing to take direction.

Making Amends Frees Us

Made direct amends to such people wherever possible, except when to do so would injure them or others. (FAA Step Nine)

Step Nine, where we make amends to ourselves and to others harmed by our addictive behavior, is not easy. But it is critical in freeing us from the negativity of the past.

In recovery, I am responsible to do all I can to right the wrongs of my past. I begin with my Fifth Step by admitting my misdeeds to myself, to God, and to another human being. I eventually make amends to the person I had harmed. Amends might include paying back money I owe or making a formal apology, perhaps even publicly. It might entail actively working to improve all aspects of a relationship.

Making amends above all means change. I grieve for my misguided past and turn away from that way of life. And I continue to make amends as needed in accordance with this new happy, free, and useful way of life.

For today, I ask my Higher Power to guide me as I make amends.

Good Orderly Direction

When we head down a dangerous path, our Higher Power alerts us with a gentle nudge – perhaps a phone call from a friend that alters our thoughts of bingeing.

If we ignore the subtle signals that arise from within us and instead forge ahead toward self-destruction, the signals get stronger – our heart may race or our stomach may tighten.

What does it take to get abstinent? Many of us had to experience extreme hopelessness or perhaps the drawn-out misery of off-and-on abstinence. All of us have suffered from this disease. When we finally learn to listen to our Higher Power, our misery is lifted.

We now know to heed the gentle nudge each time we veer off track. We no longer need to wander down the deadly path of food addiction, ignoring the taps and pushes that we are given. We can learn from each misstep we have taken and continue on our journey.

We seek to remain open and teachable, so that the gentle nudges that we receive are all that it takes to keep us on the straight and narrow.

For today, I ask God to keep me attuned to those gentle nudges.

Courage to Change

God, grant me the serenity to accept the things I cannot change, courage to change the things I can and the wisdom to know the difference. (The Serenity Prayer)

In the Serenity Prayer, I ask for the courage to change the things I can. What are those things? In my addiction, I may have believed that I was all-powerful and knew what was best for everyone. If only they would follow my advice, everyone would be happy and all would be right with the world.

At times I may have believed that I was weak and could not change a thing. I couldn't change my thoughts or feelings or my outlook on life.

With the help of FAA and through working the Steps, I am now learning what things I can change. I can change my behavior, my choices, and the approach I take to life. I cannot change the world around me, but I can change the world inside me.

For today, I turn my life and my will over to God and focus on becoming the person that my Higher Power wants me to be.

Accepting Myself

There are moments of reflection when I wish I were somewhere else in life or had accomplished something greater. I may regret decisions I have made or actions I have taken and the consequences of those decisions and actions. A good thing to remember at these times is that I am only where I am able to be.

Events in my life have molded me. I made regrettable decisions because of my upbringing or because of the disease of food addiction. I am only human, and I have faults that have contributed to the bad things in my life.

Instead of looking backward, I can look to where I want to be. Today I am exactly where I need to be.

I am who I am. In recovery, I am much less self-conscious. I know today that I have flaws, but I am not the focus of everyone else's attention. I am satisfied with who I am and accept others as they are as well.

Today I do not have to be anyone but me. I enjoy my imperfections. The more that I'm willing to reveal my flaws, the more positively people respond to me.

For today, I ask for the confidence to present myself to the world exactly as I am.

Willingness

We have committed to living in recovery just for today. Each day when we arise, we need only be concerned with our next meal, not a lifetime of meals.

We can maintain an attitude of gratitude by reminding ourselves of how good it feels to be abstinent. We can now enjoy the little things in life, like shopping for food that supports our abstinence, chatting with a friend, or walking in the park. We feel more love for the people in our lives.

Each time we relapse, things get worse. The result is always the same: guilt, self-hate, shame, isolation, depression, and suicidal thoughts. Conversely, when we are abstinent, we know that today is a good day, despite what ever else is going on in our lives.

We begin to see where we belong in this world – where our talents and passions can best be used. We may be afraid, but we put our trust in God. We begin to feel God's love and forgiveness.

Now I can be responsible for my actions because I am abstinent.

For today, I ask God for the willingness to be abstinent this one day.

Eating is Not the Quick Fix

Many of us choose the path of least resistance and stay in our pain and insanity rather than risk temporary discomfort on the way to a more lasting recovery.

As a food addict, I have a tendency to believe that what is going on with my body (tiredness, dizziness, etc.) will be affected if I eat more or eat less. I've spent years using all sorts of reasons to change my food and change my daily eating plan. The result was always the same – insanity.

Sometimes I'd think that eating more was the answer; other times, eating less. And eating less had the added attraction of weight loss. "This can't possibly be the disease," I thought, "because I'm losing weight."

Unfortunately, this kind of thinking is not uncommon. The disease will go to any lengths to become active again. One of its tricks is to make us think that if we don't eat all the food we committed to our sponsor, it's not a big deal. Today I know that messing around with the food plan is always a sign of disease, not recovery. I have to make a decision between recovery and disease.

I will no longer be a victim. I choose to trust the process as related to me by other food addicts in recovery.

For today, I thank God for the courage and power to make new life-affirming choices.

Staying Abstinent Today

When I awaken in the morning, I can pray for the knowledge of God's will for me and the power to carry it out. I can thank God for my abstinence. I can read a meditation, do some writing, and call my sponsor.

During the day, I can make phone calls to fellow FAA members or read what's on the FAA loop. I can attend a meeting in person, online, or by phone. I can plan and prepare my food for the next day.

I can do something just for me, even if it's five minutes of quiet time, just to breathe. I can get enough sleep.

I don't have to do any of these things perfectly, but I can do them consistently. I can be rigorously honest with my sponsor, leaving nothing out about my food for that day. I do not omit any information regarding any diversions from what I had committed on my food plan.

By the grace of God, these actions will keep me abstinent for another 24 hours.

For today, I utilize every tool at my disposal to remain abstinent.

It's More than "I'm Sorry"

Making direct amends to the people who have suffered because of my disease – myself included – tops the list of actions required in Step Nine. Lying, stealing, and manipulating people and events to get my fix are uncovered in my moral inventory.

Minimization, rationalization, and justification were ways I tried to deal with the effect of my food addiction on my relationships. I was not there for my family and friends. I could not identify and meet my own needs. I had distanced myself from God. I made many choices that harmed people.

In recovery, I am responsible to do all I can to right the wrongs of my past. I make amends to the people I have hurt unless it would cause further harm. This may include paying back money I owe, making a public apology, actively working on improving all aspects of the relationship, and realigning my priorities. It definitely means change! Just apologizing is only the beginning. I continue to make living amends, one day at a time.

For today, I ask my Higher Power to continue to show me the amends I need to make and to give me the willingness to make them.

There is Only This Moment

I have to work the program only one moment at a time. A gift of my early abstinence was the decision to delay. It meant confronting the urge or craving and then deciding, "No, at this moment I am not going to eat that."

I learned I do not have to wallow in grief because I will never eat my former favorite foods. I confidently affirm my plan for today. Being in the moment means I gain energy and room to take in the delights of this day. Acknowledging that I don't know what tomorrow holds helps me stay humble.

Living one moment at a time, I can let go of romancing my past. By using the Twelve Steps, I look at my past to learn patterns. I no longer need to linger and relive the painful memories of shame, guilt, anger, fear, and loneliness that characterized my active food addiction. When I choose to stay in the moment, I may even feel gratitude that I know the truth about my body and addictive foods.

For today, I ask my Higher Power to help me to be present in each moment, each meal, and each bite.

The Pay-Off for Recovery

To recover from food addiction, I must surrender to abstinence and to working the program. This requires a leap of faith at first. But the gifts bestowed in return for my willingness are endless. As these blessings flow into my life, my resistance lessens, surrender deepens, and gratitude soon fills my heart.

Physically, my body begins to heal. My mind grows steady. Intellect and memory sharpen. Creative energy flows. I develop solid self-esteem and the ability to care for myself and assert boundaries. I am present and alert around others.

The spiritual void within begins to fill. I develop a loving relationship with a Higher Power who supports me absolutely and passionately in this new way of life. I let go of the past. I no longer judge the world or myself harshly. I accept each moment as given by the God of my understanding as part of this marvelous journey. I know peace.

These are The Promises listed in Step Nine that so many of us have realized and so many more are discovering. With surrender, persistence, and faith, practiced one day at a time, our lives will gently flower to the full warmth and radiance of serene recovery.

For today, I acknowledge all The Promises that have come true in my life.

Compassion for Myself

I often binged on sugar, flour, and wheat to stuff my feelings and numb myself. I hated who I was and tried in vain to escape. I just couldn't stand being me anymore.

I know today that eating addictively is an act of self-abuse. As I remain abstinent, I turn self-abuse into self-nurturing. I have more compassion for myself. I love myself and trust my instincts. I let go of shame and fill myself with good thoughts and feelings. I embrace my struggles, knowing that they are getting me to a better place. I accept my needs and wants as genuine and important. I am not a nuisance – I am a precious creation.

The key to nurturing me is to follow the FAA food plan. I avoid sugar, flour, and wheat in all their forms and weigh and measure my meals. Following this suggested food plan is not a punishment. It is an act of compassion toward myself.

For today, I choose to love, care for, and nurture myself.

Letting Go of Obsession

With abstinence, I am relieved of the obsession with sugar, flour, and wheat. Then other obsessions are uncovered. I may become obsessed with weight, exercise, money, shopping or any number of things. I have learned that obsession with anything eventually leads back to the food. Because anything that I obsess about works me into a frenzy, and, as a food addict, I know that my disease will tell me that the food will relieve me.

Obsession keeps me holding on to something that I hope will make me sane. But usually anything that I think will make me sane ends up making me feel insane.

I no longer have a need to grasp for something that I know will slip away. When I notice my thoughts becoming diseased, I can call a fellow FAA member, pray, read a piece of literature, write, or do service. Once I pick up a tool, I can let go of the obsession. It doesn't take long for sanity to be restored.

The FAA program, the fellowship, and the spirit therein are the antidotes to the flimsy rope of obsession.

For today, I seek balance in my thoughts and life.

Emotional Maturity

With abstinence, I get the opportunity to feel my feelings. I can use the following 4-word checklist to review how I am doing emotionally:

- *Anger* equals the feeling I get when I don't get my way today.
- *Resentment* equals the feeling I get when I think about having not gotten my way yesterday.
- *Fear* equals the feeling I get when I worry that I won't get my way tomorrow.
- *Depression* equals the feeling I get when I sit around wondering why I never get my way.

Before I found FAA, I reacted to the world as a child does. I insisted on getting my own way. I wanted what I wanted when I wanted it. To quell my feelings of anger, resentment, fear, and depression, I ate.

Today childish reactions are replaced with spiritual tools. My recovery depends on my seeking through prayer and meditation the knowledge of God's will for me and the power to carry it out. I am willing to give up wanting what I want in order to find the peace and serenity of emotional maturity.

For today, I continue to seek the peace that comes with emotional maturity.

More Isn't Always Better

A common mindset with food addicts is that more is better.

Our disease tries to convince us that if we ate just a little more, we would be satisfied. We weren't. Most of us have discovered that our full mechanism has been broken for a very long time.

Our disease tries to convince us that if we just put on more weight and got fat enough, then surely we would stop eating. We didn't. We continued to put on pound after pound, passing numbers on the scale that we swore we would never reach. Despite our best efforts, we continued to gain weight.

Our disease tries to convince us that if we just lose some more weight then we'll feel better. We didn't. We may have starved ourselves or exercised to an extreme and damaged our bodies in the process. More loss was really too much loss and was unhealthy.

We have found that maintaining a regimen of eating weighed and measured meals offers us the "more" that had eluded us. We find that the only real "more" that truly makes us feel better is more abstinence. It is only through abstinence that we find real freedom, satisfaction, and serenity.

For today, I ask God to give me the wisdom to realize that more isn't better except when I am counting my days of abstinence.

Identifying Feelings

When we are in active addiction, we find that we have two basic feelings: miserable and numb. We often have no idea of the feelings underneath.

After we have lived awhile in abstinence, we begin to recognize our long-hidden feelings as they rise to the surface. Our task as recovering food addicts is to identify those feelings.

Once we are able to identify our feelings, we can look at the thoughts that led to those feelings. For example, we may be able to recall an incident that made us angry but that, in the food, was expressed as depression. We may identify resentments that were in fact fostered by our unrealistic expectations.

When we explore our thoughts and feelings, we let go of self-condemnation and find that we are developing a sense of maturity and growth.

We learn other ways of thinking, and then we build on those healthier thoughts and reinforce them. We begin to believe that we deserve recovery, and because we come to believe this wholeheartedly, it becomes our reality.

For today, I explore my feelings and thoughts and choose healthy ways in which to deal with them.

Seeking My Truth

Perhaps we came from the generation that believed "Children should be seen, not heard" and "Speak when spoken to." We may have gotten the message early on that no one wanted to hear our voice.

As children we probably had so much to say but were told, "You don't really feel that way" or "No one feels like that." Soon we learned to question our own thoughts and feelings. We learned to stuff our feelings and quiet our voices with sugar. We learned to feed our bodies while hiding our reality. We grew up to become adults with no sense of self.

In FAA we gave up sugar, flour, and wheat and began to speak our truth. What we used to think were hunger pains we now know are our gut feelings. We ask God to show us how to be honest. We begin to recognize our feelings and speak them. In FAA we find not only that God listens to our hearts and feelings but that there are so many food addicts who really care about who we are, how we feel and what we do.

For today, I ask my Higher Power for courage to speak my own truth.

It's All There

We tell the newcomers in the meetings about the Food Plan and the Steps, but it seems little is said about the Twelve Traditions. Whether we are aware of it or not, we actually introduce newcomers to the Traditions.

At the very first meeting, we hold out our hands and say, "If you want to stop eating addictive foods, you're welcome, no matter who you are or what you weigh." (Tradition Three).

We offer phone numbers and literature and share experiences of what helped us most in the beginning (Tradition Five).We reassure frightened newcomers that their secrets and their membership are safe with us (Tradition Twelve). We offer a safe haven, where abstinence is the only issue and there are no strings attached as we have no opinion on outside issues (Tradition Ten), fully self-supporting, declining outside contributions (Tradition Seven) and we also have no outside affiliations, lest problems of money, property and prestige divert us from our primary purpose (Tradition Six).

Following the Traditions on an individual level is the foundation for following them on a group level and provides unity and strength to FAA(Tradition Two).

For today, I thank my Higher Power for the wisdom of the Twelve Traditions.

Letting Go of Resentments

Resentments are toxic to my system. Over and over in my head, I replay a scene. Over and over, I obsess on another's imagined wrongs against me. Over and over, I plot a course of action in which I get even and come out on top. Over and over and over and over is an unhealthy state of mind for me today.

Resentments keep me out of the moment. If I am living in the past, I am living in negativity. It is like taking poison. As a food addict, I cannot afford resentments. Allowing resentments to fester in my mind is the equivalent of putting flour, sugar, and wheat into my body.

How do I let go of my resentments? I can talk to another FAA member. I can pray for the person for whom I feel resentment. I can reach out to a newcomer. I can take a positive action. What I cannot do is hold on to these venomous thoughts.

For today, I let go of my resentments that endanger my abstinence.

Which Voice?

Inside of me I have a demanding 4-year-old who does not necessarily know what is good for her. This child succumbs to lies offered up by the disease. Lies like I can eat one doughnut or one piece of chocolate. Lies that I will never be slender and healthy and that I might as well just give up trying. Lies that tell me that some people are born fat and that neither God nor FAA nor anyone else can change that.

I know the truth. I know that my disease lies. I also know the truth about recovery. I know that God offers me recovery. For me, that recovery is through the healing power of FAA. I know that I will always be given help if I reach out and use my tools.

I have to decide which voice I want to listen to – the vulnerable 4-year old, the disease, or the loving and kind voice of recovery that draws me closer and closer to miracle after miracle in my life.

For today, I listen for the truth of the message from God as I understand God, active and alive in my life.

Sponsor and Sponsee

On the days that my food addiction tells me to isolate and to avoid reaching out to anybody, I pray to my Higher Power for the strength to share my feelings. On the days that my food addiction tells me that I don't need to work the Steps or follow the FAA food plan, I pray to my Higher Power for the courage to call my sponsor and share what is going on in my life.

I know that I can safely share and express my feelings because my sponsor is just another food addict going through the recovery process just like me, one day at a time. My disease taught me that it was not safe to share my feelings or express them to another person. My disease taught me to hide my true self. I had lost the ability to know my feelings and thoughts. Sugar, flour, and wheat not only gummed up my body but my mind as well.

As long as I am abstinent, I have the clarity to make sound and practical choices for myself. A vital part of my recovery today is making that phone call. I know that I may not hear the answers I am looking for but, with abstinence, I know that I will hear what I need.

For today, I keep myself open to hear my sponsor's wisdom.

No Longer Afraid

I have lived most of my life afraid of people. I would compare myself to others, and I always fell short of what I thought other people thought I should be. I would imagine that other people were looking at me and judging everything about me. I felt I had nothing to give others. I would freeze up and become tongue-tied at work or in social situations. I never felt okay and I never thought I would fit in anywhere. This made my life miserable.

FAA has taught me to accept myself as I am and to allow God to make the changes in my life that will help me to carry the message to other food addicts. The love that has been offered to me in FAA has started to heal my fractured soul. It has allowed me to give and receive love in a way that I have not been able to experience before.

I know that I am cared about, supported, and given strength and hope every day. The promises are coming true minute by minute.

For today, I celebrate who and what I am. I am enough.

Grateful Abstinence

Today I know that abstinence is a precious gift available to all of us, and for that I am grateful. I can't pay lip service to gratitude. Gratitude means sharing this gift with others. Gratitude is an action word. Gratitude means giving back to the fellowship that has given me so much. Lip service is what I gave to the food that was killing me for so many years.

I know that if I am ever to keep the quality of life that abstinence and the program have given me, I must carry the message to other suffering food addicts. It is then that it will multiply in my life as well as in the lives of others. I can't keep it if I don't give it away.

For today, I choose to put my recovery into action and will share both the program and my gratitude with at least one other food addict.

Recovery Changes Our Thinking

We have a disease, that when active, causes us to behave in ways that are not positive to those around us or to ourselves. Rather than focus on what is bad in each other, we can focus on what is good. And through the FAA program, we learn that a person is more than the behavior he or she exhibits.

In recovery we behave differently and see things in a more positive light. The negativity is lifted and we are left feeling better and in tune with our true selves as well as with those around us. We do not judge others. Instead, we ask to be shown what we can learn from them.

All things are possible when we choose abstinence, have faith in the program, and live a life in recovery.

For today, I walk the path of recovery, seeing the good in others as well as in myself.

Discovering the Real Me

When I first came into the meeting rooms I had no idea who or what I was: all I could feel was the pain and shame caused by my eating behaviors. I was sick, I was scared, and I knew I could not continue to blindly stuff my pain with food. Taking a leap of faith to attend that first FAA meeting saved my life and my soul.

Acknowledging that food helped me survive a childhood filled with pain led me to the next step in my recovery: letting go of my "best friends"– sugar, flour, and wheat. When I let go of my addictive substances and let God in, I was able to work through old hurts and bravely face my character defects.

When I get impatient with my progress, I remind myself that recovery is a process of peeling away and discarding the layers of dysfunction to uncover the real me. At times, my efforts can feel painful, as the disparaging voices in my head try desperately to keep their dominant position in dictating my behaviors. Relief fills me as I reach for the tools of the program and allow my Higher Power to lead me out of the darkness.

For today, I ask my Higher Power for an abundance of patience as I gradually discover who I really am.

God's Love

When I am in despair and cannot hold it together any longer – when I have put on my recovery face long enough – when I have used the tools ad nauseam – when I lose it and cry out to God, God is there. I cry out "Help me" and God helps me.

I take a small action, powered by willingness provided by God. I pick up the phone and call someone who will help. I pick up a book that happens to have the perfect words for calming me down.

In God's infinite love, wisdom, and power, God guides me to the next sane action, which in turn shifts me into the next sane thought. And I finally get a grip again.

For today, I reach out to God for a way toward peace, serenity, and joy.

Taking Responsibility for My Actions

Made direct amends to such people wherever possible except when to do so would injure them or others. (FAA Step Nine)

How do I make direct amends to the people I have harmed? I have my Eighth Step list. Where do I start? The "wherever possible" is the key.

I need to search my motives for making amends to ensure that I don't do more harm than good. I become willing to forgo hearing "I am sorry too." My behavior caused the harm and I am willing to take responsibility for it.

Amends are about me being accountable for my actions and repairing relationships where I can, always remembering that God is at the center.

For today, I continue to make direct amends when wrong and am grateful for guidance from my Higher Power.

Using the Tools for Deeper Insight

Go to a meeting. Share. Make phone calls. Be honest. These are activities and attitudes we are taught in the program. We are given plenty of opportunity to rid ourselves of our painful secrets in order to heal from them.

In addition, we have tools, such as writing, sponsorship, fellowship, prayer, and meditation, to further enhance our recovery.

Sometimes we may feel that we are not being genuine with others. We may be putting on our recovery face at a meeting in order to fit in. We may not always share the truth about ourselves. This is where the other tools can be most beneficial. Writing, for example, can be very therapeutic, and no one else ever needs to see it. Prayer and meditation can bring us honestly and humbly to God, when we are too angry or scared to face other people.

The FAA tools of recovery help us uncover our true selves and help us to embrace that person. As we use all of the tools at our disposal, we begin to like ourselves more and more and gain confidence in who we are. We find the courage to be true to ourselves and, in turn, true to others.

For today, I pick up my tools to strengthen my recovery.

Faithfulness

This program brings a completely new meaning to the word faith. Through working the Twelve Steps in a serious, committed way, we forge a relationship with God that changes our lives. The big empty hole that we used to try to fill with food now is filled with faith. We gain faith in place of the doubt, fear, anxiety, and lack of trust that once ruled our lives.

While we are relieved of many of our character defects, we may still struggle with others. We can accept with faith that there is a plan and the character defects that remain will be removed in God's time.

For today, I look at all the ways in which my faith has grown since I became willing to trust the Twelve Step process.

Healthy Choices

When I came into Food Addicts Anonymous, my life was in turmoil, my food was out of control, my mind was confused, and my soul was empty. Naturally, with all this going on, my self-esteem was on the floor. Maybe my way of compensating for this was perpetual overachieving. I had to do, do, do in the hopes that you would like me. If I showed you what I was capable of accomplishing, it might raise my worth in your eyes. I needed approval. Underneath my happy facade, I felt worthless and unworthy of love.

Abstinence has changed the way I feel. As I get my food in order, one of the positve side effects is that I feel better about myself. As I progress in my recovery, I want to practice more healthy, self-nurturing behaviors. And the more I do these things, the better I feel about myself.

With abstinence, the sky's the limit.

For today, I nurture myself knowing that I am loved just as I am.

Tenth Step Evaluations

Continued to take personal inventory, and when we were wrong, promptly admitted it. (FAA Step Ten)

In working Step Ten, we routinely take note of mistakes that we have made and consider how to avoid repeating them. We ask for our sponsor's advice if we are unsure of how to address a problem. We keep in mind that we do not make amends if it would injure that person or others. And we promptly admit when we are wrong.

We also consider our worthy acts each day to counter any tendency to accumulate and dwell on self-critical thoughts. We can consider specific examples of how we showed up for the day, met responsibilities, worked the program, stayed abstinent, and interacted well with the people in our lives. We note areas of progress. This part of our inventory keeps us aware and grateful that in abstinence our lives are happy, sane, and useful.

"Know thyself" is a motto of recovery. The Tenth Step reminds us to continually evaluate who we are, what we are doing, and where we are going. It gives us good orderly direction as we refine the art of living a joyful life.

For today, I let God guide me as I review my thoughts and actions.

Spiritual Responsibility

One of our most basic needs as human beings is spiritual – the need for the spiritual resources and power that will allow us to live good lives. There is no spiritual need that our Higher Power cannot meet. And FAA is a spiritual program that allows us to make contact with our Higher Power.

We consistently receive the power that we need when we seek to give it freely to others. Our Higher Power strengthens us as we share what we have with people who need our help. This strength leads to better health, better relationships, and more satisfying work. We can then help more and more people. And so it continues.

Our spiritual needs are met as we allow our Higher Power to work through us.

For today, I trust that my Higher Power meets all of my spiritual needs.

The Gift of Me

If through abstinence we have shed many pounds or have increased our body weight to reflect good health, our friends and family may have commented that we have become unrecognizable.

Sometimes when we lose a lot of weight, people even remark that we have lost a whole person. The truth is, however, that we have gained a whole person. We have gained ourselves.

Before FAA, many of us felt like an empty shell. We kept trying to fill that empty shell with something, usually sugar, flour, and wheat. We became increasingly fatter, sadder, and emptier inside.

Having searched for so long, we value this precious discovery of ourselves. We now take loving care of ourselves. We live our lives to the fullest. Like a child, we explore, reaching out to try new things. Sometimes we succeed, sometimes we don't. But we are always learning, growing, and immensely enjoying this new life.

For today, I cherish having found myself. I use my recovery tools so that I may hold on to this precious gift.

The Payoff

The joys of recovery are not discovered until a leap of faith and surrender to this program have been accomplished.

Many of us may have feared abstinence for a number of years because the cost of giving up our trigger foods seemed so great. We could not imagine life without them. They had been our joy, our god, our comfort. We kept denying the fact that they were crippling us, both physically and emotionally.

When we finally surrendered, we quit arguing, regardless of our opinions and beliefs. When we truly listened to another FAA member who had what we wanted, we were able to see that what was being asked of us was so much less than what we would receive.

The payoff for surrendering "our way" enriches our lives with countless miracles daily. With abstinence, even the smallest miracle and awareness brings us abundant joy.

For today, I listen to my Higher Power and follow the examples of other recovering food addicts.

Give up the Struggle

Some of us have experienced a high level of serenity at a retreat or convention. Several days of making our food planning and our spiritual program our top priority shifted our struggle. Perhaps we returned home with our tension and fear relieved. For some of us our first few meals were effortless, with no desire to eat any extra bites. It was a natural, flowing peace, with no resistant voices in our head. What a relief it was to let go, to completely surrender.

Yet at any point, our self-will can raise its ugly head. We can take in a little more food here and there. We cut short our prayer and meditation time and lose our peace, even if we are abstinent.

We can remember in difficult times that we never have to struggle because we have a Higher Power.

For today, I ask God to help me remember that my struggles can be shifted by simply asking for help.

Recovery Comes First

Food Addicts Anonymous has no opinion on outside issues; hence the FAA name ought never be drawn into public controversy. (FAA Tradition Ten)

We came to FAA because of food addiction. This commonality binds us. Our singleness of purpose frees us as a group from engaging in outside activities or causes, no matter how worthwhile or related they may seem.

Those who have come before us strived to preserve the integrity of FAA. This precious fellowship has been a safe harbor for countless food addicts for many years. None of us wants to destroy it. Yet this is exactly what we would do if we allow the name Food Addicts Anonymous to be associated with any outside issue.

It is up to each of us to be mindful of preserving FAA so that we will always have a place to go. By keeping the focus on our primary spiritual aim, we can continue to have this program as a sanctuary from the disease of food addiction. There is a time and a place for controversy on politics, religion or other social issues, but the time and place is not in our fellowship.

For today, I remember to apply Tradition Ten to my life – controversy and serenity don't mix.

Guarding Abstinence

Going to any lengths to keep my abstinence is my number one goal for the day and the measure of my recovery. Some FAA members are able to regain their abstinence quickly, but others are not. It is humbling to realize the power of this disease. Going to any lengths means:

- Making time to stock up on my needed foods
- Making time to cook meals for the days ahead
- Committing my food to my sponsor every day
- Keeping the food plan handy so that I can see what I need for the next meal
- Sometimes eating foods that are not my favorites
- Keeping spiritually fit with literature, prayer, and meditation
- Asking for help when I need it

This is how I guard my abstinence. In fact, there are times when I have to grasp even more tools. I call another recovering food addict and take his or her direction on what I should do next – new behavior for me, as I was always "self-sufficient." But I remember that self-sufficiency almost cost me my life.

For today, I take directions needed to ensure my abstinence.

Respecting Boundaries

As addicts, we have particular weaknesses regarding relationships. In recovery, we learn to establish personal boundaries. We learn where we end and where others begin. We learn to define clearly our obligations and commitments to others. We learn the tactful art of agreeing on limitations to maintain peaceful relations. We become comfortable with clearly establishing our bottom line.

Once we establish our boundaries, a daily inventory is a vital requirement in assessing our honesty and in keeping our commitments.

Trusting others and trusting ourselves is a big issue for us, so it is a very important part of our recovery. We learn to negotiate in our relationships. We learn to define our expectations and enter into commitments with caution.

Personal integrity increases as we honor ourselves. Our sense of self-worth grows as we strengthen our boundaries.

For today, I remember that my serenity lies in respecting boundaries and in honoring commitments.

Reject Diet Mentality

My Higher Power challenges my way of thinking about food and about my body. Two words keep coming to me – Diet Mentality.

When I look at my history with my food addiction, I realize that I was thinking in terms of weight loss rather than recovery from food addiction. When I think in terms of how I look instead of being free from the obsession with food, I am in diet mentality. If I allow even one small hope to linger that a new and better diet is lurking around the corner, I'm off the recovery path.

There is a simple way to judge whether I am engaged in diet mentality. Am I willing to follow the food plan and program to the best of my ability and not focus on weight loss? Am I willing to look at the food plan as a plan for healing my body and view weight loss as a by-product of it? If I am, then I'm in recovery and not in diet mentality. I am free from the burden of dieting.

For today, I ask to remain willing and teachable. I rely on the wisdom of other recovering food addicts to help me recognize faulty thinking.

Planning Prevents Poor Performance

The Guide to Abstinence reminds us that prior planning prevents poor performance. Planning is a big part of our recovery. It is incredibly important to know when we will eat, what we will eat, and how much we will eat. In the beginning, weighing, measuring, and label-reading may seem too much – too rigid, too restrictive, too legalistic, just too much! However, in the doing comes the understanding.

We learn that by taking the action, our feelings and then our attitudes change. We can be fearful and still take the action of not eating addictive food and sticking to the food plan. We can remember that we are not doing this alone. We have sponsors and fellow recovering food addicts to call who will help us with our planning. They are happy to share with us how they organize their food and preparation time. We become willing to reach out to them as we become more and more aware that our way didn't work. We are all only one bite away from insanity.

For today, I remember that if I fail to plan, then I have planned to fail.

Guided By the Steps

I am on a spiritual path, recovering one day at a time and finding a healthier and saner way of living. What amazing things God has in store for us as we become willing and open to receive these gifts.

Step One tells me that I have a problem, Step Two says that I have a Higher Power who has the solution, and Step Three says that I turn my will and my life over to that Higher Power.

I become willing to surrender foods that are not good for me. When I stray from the food plan, I also stray from my Higher Power. I am then making binge foods my higher power because that's what I'm turning to in times of difficulty.

Surrender is throwing up my hands and saying, "God, you take control. I am relinquishing the driver's seat." I may fall along the way, but I know that I will get back up. God will do for me what I can't do for myself, if I allow it. God needs my cooperation.

Surrender is becoming easier now that I can say that my way doesn't work.

For today, I ask my Higher Power to help me appreciate the spiritual lessons I am learning by staying abstinent and following the FAA program.

Promptly Taking Action

The Twelve Step way of life is simple but not easy. Steps One, Five, and Ten ask us to admit something. In Step One it's our powerlessness. Step Five asks us to admit to God, ourselves, and another human being the exact nature of our wrongs. There is no enforced time frame in these Steps. However, in Step Ten there is. It asks us to promptly admit when we are wrong.

Step Ten also suggests that we continue to take a moral inventory, implying that we will probably not be perfect at avoiding stepping on the toes of others. It would be too easy to put off making the amends. When problems arise I ask my Higher Power to show me my part. I will then ask God to give me the willingness to promptly say those three most difficult words: "I am sorry."

For today, I begin the daily practice of doing a Tenth Step Inventory.

Accentuate the Positive

It may be difficult to break a long-established pattern of complaining and whining, but it's certainly worth the effort. As I continue to work the Steps and remain abstinent, I begin to realize how my negative thinking has kept me a prisoner of this disease.

In the past, I rarely trusted or acknowledged my feelings or knew what to do or how to react in an adult manner. The Twelve Steps and the FAA fellowship are teaching me how to react and respond in a healthy, mature, positive way.

As I continue to attend meetings, it becomes easier and more natural for me to look for the positive, not only in others, but also in myself.

I am grateful to have the clarity that abstinence brings, including recognizing unacceptable behavior in myself and in others.

For today, I will replace a negative attitude with a positive one.

Never Enough

Day after day on this journey, the layers of delusion continue to shed. I discover more and more truths about myself.

One truth that has become clear is that when I chase after anything but God, I can never get enough. I can never have enough of what is not good for me.

No matter what I weigh, how much I exercise, how I look, who is in my life, what job I have, or where I live, it is never enough to fill me up.

Only God can fill me. Everything else is an unsatisfying substitute that sets me up for craving more. Repeated mistakes and hard-earned lessons show me that God is all I need.

The more I connect with my Higher Power through service, prayer, and meditation, the more God I get. And knowing God is the only way that I can ever feel that I have enough.

A yearning for something more is part of the human condition. I needn't run from it. The answer to that yearning, God's love, is something that I already have. I need only open my heart and let it in.

For today, I will pray to be open to receiving God's love and guidance.

A New Set of Tools

I've acquired a new set of tools. The old ones, myriad ways of combining sugar, flour, and wheat, were worn out and terribly hazardous. Addictive eating was a blunt and awkward response to life, knocking me unconscious with a flood of serotonin to temporarily relieve my emotional discomfort. I just knew there had to be a better way. My new tools are finely honed, light, and easy to wield. With abstinence as my foundation I have never hurt myself using these new tools:

- Self-care and adequate rest smooth the rough edges
- The Steps guide me through tangled emotional undergrowth
- Meetings, telephone, and service work build a bridge to the community
- Faith and trust in God wash fear away
- Prayer and meditation fill the hole in the soul
- Love, laughter, and joy power the light in my life

With my new tools, I don't have to fight. I am no longer a destroyer, but rather, an artisan who designs a life that is a masterpiece.

For today, I ask God to remind me to use my new tools as I practice this fine art of living.

The Past is Past

The day finally came when I was ready to do Step Five with my sponsor. I had written Step Four in a notebook. I had gone all the way back to my first memories. As I started to read it aloud, I had feelings of resentment, anger, fear, and shame. From time to time, I would start crying.

As I did this over and over, she would ask me questions and take notes. I learned more about the real me. I will always be grateful for the gentle but real truths that I had to face. When I had finished reading all of the pages, she asked, when did this happen? I said in the past. She smiled and told me that is where the events should stay. She told me forgiveness is remembering without resentment.

Continuing to take my inventory in Step Ten gives me the freedom to face each day as a new day, as long as I deal with the past when it reappears in my old habits and behavior.

For today, I ask God to keep me in the present moment and to recognize that my past is past.

Nurturing

Before recovery we may have thought that food was the only thing that could take away our pain and make us feel calm and cared about. But at some point food caused more pain, anxiety, and problems than we had ever imagined. Now as we recount all the gifts that this program has brought us, we affirm that it is our life in recovery that supports us and helps us to grow.

We take the time to inventory and acknowledge the good in our lives such as caring friends, restored relationships, and the ability to be responsible adults. This inventory teaches us how to love ourselves and to make good choices that move us into deeper recovery. We show others how we like to be treated by the way we treat ourselves.

There is no food that can give us what we find as we walk this spiritual path. Food is just food. Joy and peace stem from our new life.

For today, I look outside of food for what nurtures me.

Spiritual Pulse

At first glance, the Tenth Step seems like a repetition of the Fourth Step. But the Tenth Step involves more because it includes all of the spiritual growth gained from the Steps in between.

When we began our Fourth Step and faced taking a personal inventory, some of us felt overwhelmed. Yet, by taking regular inventories, it becomes almost second nature to look at our actions and our attitudes when we feel uncomfortable in a situation. We also recognize and appreciate our good qualities. This is growth.

By promptly admitting our wrongs each day, we can lovingly but firmly correct ourselves. We do not have to carry the burden of shame.

Admitting that we may be wrong takes maturity. It is reassuring to know that we can call on our Higher Power, our sponsor, and our FAA friends to help us find the strength to admit our wrongs.

That is why the Tenth Step is a joyful one. It pulls together all that we have learned in previous Steps and shows us the way to freedom.

For today, I am free to start each day with a clean slate.

The Path Through the Forest

Today I view my abstinence not as a limitation or constraint on my options, but as guidance and direction, like a path through a forest.

I had much less freedom in my food choices before abstinence. Without my food plan, my choices were largely limited to excessive quantities of foods that fueled my food addiction. This was compulsion, not choice. I would hurt myself by eating to the point of semi-consciousness and physical pain.

Lost for years in the dark forest of addiction, wandering in circles, getting nowhere, I finally stumbled across a clear path – the FAA program. Avoiding sugar, flour, wheat, and other high carbohydrate foods is avoiding the brambles, bogs, and pitfalls that kept me struggling for years. The edges of the path are not a limitation, but rather, direction, protection, and guidance out of the dark woods to freedom.

I can't always envision the light of the meadow up ahead, but I trust the reports of those who have walked before me and who gently offer their guidance to us who follow.

For today, I pray that God will remove any desire I may have to wander from this path.

No Regrets

Do you ever wish that you weren't a food addict? Perhaps you can come to trust that being a food addict is a blessing.

Do you ever wish that you had found the program earlier in life? Perhaps you can come to trust that you found the program when you were ready for it.

Do you ever wish that you had surrendered sooner? Perhaps you can trust that you could not have been any different than you were at any particular time. But now you are ready.

We need not regret the past. Each moment was necessary to bring us to where we are today. Remembering the past can help us better understand ourselves. We can leave regrets behind.

Nothing has been wasted. We are exactly where we need to be. We can embrace the moment, do the next right thing, and trust that we are on the right path. We come to see that what we thought were failures were in fact great lessons.

For today, I thank God for the lessons of the past, the gift of the present, and the promise of the future.

The Rainbow of Recovery

In the disease of food addiction, life is one even shade of gray, which grows ever darker as I linger in addiction and the disease progresses.

In abstinence, my life still has challenges, sorrows, and troubles. But I accept today that adversity is an opportunity from my Higher Power to help me grow. This is my path; I wouldn't want it any other way.

Life is not always easy. It is meant to be vibrant, colorful, free, and filled with joy. When I am abstinent and turn my life and will over to God each day, it is all of these things. I am present and experience life at its fullest. Today, I feel my feelings, both good and bad. I see the joy as well as sorrow around me, the light, as well as the darkness. I will grow, just a little, in wisdom today, as I stay present to perceive the brilliance and beauty of this rainbow of creation before me.

For today, I seek to live life on life's terms, to see all the colors of the rainbow arching over my path.

Rejuvenate With Healthy Solutions

When I have a firm spiritual foundation of recovery, even the darkest moments can be surmounted. As long as my solution is to stay abstinent, it is during those times of deep grief or pain that I am closest to my Higher Power and myself. Sometimes I need a relaxing day of quiet and reflection. Sometimes I need to avoid isolation by being with and around recovering people – a meeting, a phone call, or a walk with a friend. Sometimes, just the sunlight adds a warm spot to the bleakness in my heart.

I have lived a life trying to avoid pain at all costs. This was my primary reason to use addictive food – it was my solution to everything. I am learning through the gift of recovery and the Twelve Steps that the only way past pain is through it.

In my darkest moments, I am never alone. The stranger I once called me is becoming a dear friend. The dark night of the soul has become a gift, an open door, rather than doom and gloom. It is a time of rejuvenation with God.

For today, I am grateful for finding healthier solutions to life's problems.

Honesty Releases Guilt

This disease of addiction is a tricky one. It keeps me from being honest. Then, when I am dishonest, it tells me to feel guilty.

Honesty furthers my recovery from food addiction. I do not use it to beat myself up with shame and guilt over past mistakes. Honesty is about going forward, not about reliving the past. Honesty says, "Here's what I did and here's what I'm going to do now."

I continue to be amazed by how far I've come and how much further I have to go. It's exciting, not overwhelming. My recovery just happens. All I do is follow the instructions. The instructions I've been given involve committing my food to my sponsor every day and reporting any changes I've made the previous day. Why? Because it works. This behavior keeps me honest and with honesty, there is less room for the disease to step in.

Food planning, reporting, and committing are tools that keep me from relapsing. By working the Sixth and Seventh Steps, I humbly ask my Higher Power to remove my dishonesty.

For today, I ask God to keep me honest in all my affairs, no matter how uncomfortable I may feel.

Abstinence Brings Me Happiness

Today I am abstinent. Abstinence opens the door and by working the Twelve Steps, I experience happiness. I rejoice today for the time I have been given and live today as if it's my best and only day to live.

I may need to reveal parts of me that I have learned to protect because of past feelings of rejection or failure. Sometimes such revelation gives me the wings to fly.

Today I am getting reacquainted with myself. I retreat from the daily noise of life and look within. I follow my heart, because it knows the way to go. As I tune out distractions, I hear the words I need to hear. I must face my fears and dreams today, so that I may achieve my heart's desire and fulfill my innermost wishes. I find happiness not in those things that I postpone, but in those things that I embrace today.

For today, I take the time to find a quiet place and listen to the voice of happiness.

From Denial to Acceptance

For years I denied who I was and made every attempt to become a normal eater. I wanted desperately to be a person who could eat only when hungry and stop when full, with no limitation on foods I craved.

I went to workshops and filled up dozens of notebooks with my problems. I joined fat-acceptance organizations and bought big, beautiful clothes. I read every book I could on eating disorders, compulsive eating, and weight control. I could not act on what I read, because I was an active food addict, eating substances on a daily basis that were altering my brain and body chemistry at a level that was crippling me from making any progress.

Accepting that I was a food addict began with accepting that this is a biochemical disease. The food addiction had been a heavy black curtain pulled down over a radiant existence. With abstinence, the curtain began to lift. I started to see, feel, smell, and sense the light coming from beneath the curtain. I began to feel hope. I came to believe that recovery from food addiction is part of God's purpose for my life.

With abstinence, the curtain continues to rise, and the gifts continue to come.

For today, I am accepting and grateful that I found the answer to my food addiction in the rooms of FAA.

My Concept Changes

What did I want when I first came to FAA?

Primarily, I wanted weight loss. I focused on the weight. I was gently reminded that this program is about recovery, not weight. I had to learn to be patient and to trust the process. I began to believe that if I remained abstinent I would get to the weight that God intended for me.

An old-timer at the meeting said that if you focus on weight, you lose recovery; but if you focus on recovery, you lose weight. What a concept! Today, because I have focused on recovery, I am blessed to feel good in this body and in this mind. I no longer obsess about weight and weight loss. I know that it is a part of the gifts of this program.

For today, I give thanks for the freedom from obsessing about weight loss and focus on the life recovery has made possible for me.

Footwork for Abstinence

Abstinence isn't handed to us on a silver platter. Once our Higher Power gives us the willingness to let go of our addictive substances, it's up to us to do the footwork. Sometimes, that footwork includes using the tools to counteract any negative thoughts that come to mind.

For some of us, the disease taunts us from time to time, telling us that the shopping, the cooking, the planning, and the meetings are too time-consuming. What the disease never tells us, however, is that we each have a Higher Power with us at all times. Perhaps this is our most valuable tool. With our Higher Power, we can face any event or feeling without picking up sugar, flour, wheat, or volume. All we have to do is turn over our thoughts and ask for help.

The footwork that we do to maintain abstinence is a path that we are on for the rest of our lives. But we don't travel this path alone. We have each other and we have our Higher Power right alongside us.

For today, I am grateful my Higher Power joins me on my road to recovery.

Simplicity Offers Hope

I can't. God can. I'll let God. This is shorthand for the first three Steps.

How simple this program is. All I need to do is accept my powerlessness over the disease of food addiction, find a Higher Power, and turn my life over to my Higher Power.

I begin by being honest with myself about my disease. My denial needs to be confronted and retired. I need to face the reality on a daily basis that this disease is deadly.

In working the first three Steps, I discovered that there is hope. My Higher Power removed my obsession with sugar, flour, and wheat. All I needed to do was ask, even if I did not really believe. Hope is the key that unlocks my resistance to believing in the miracle of recovery. Each day I decide whether I want to be in charge or let my Higher Power take over. In the beginning, I did not have the faith to give the reins to my Higher Power, but over time I have found that turning it over is easier than me being in control.

For today, I welcome the freedom of letting my Higher Power direct my thinking.

God's Calming Power

I was trying to dress my toddler grandson one day. He was in no mood to be dressed and fought each attempt I made to put on his clothes. At one point I was trying to put on his shirt. He tore the shirt out of my hand and insisted on trying to put the shirt sleeve over his head. As I tried to help him, he pushed my hands away and screamed louder and louder. Finally, exhausted, he looked up through the stretched sleeve and relaxed his body. He was saying, OK – you can help me now. I took the shirt and he became cooperative and loving as he allowed me to dress him. When we were finished, he gave me a big kiss and hug.

This little event made me think of how much a loving God wants to help me, and how I sometimes behave like a rebellious child fighting for no reason except to fight. In the process I hurt myself and others. When I relax, God's power can reach in and help me. I realize now that there are some rules in the universe. One of them is that God will not fight with me and force a way into my life until I ask. God can work best when I become calm, quiet, and trusting.

For today, I calm my mind and heart and ask God to work within me.

Let God Be God

I have lived most of my life feeling as though I had to be in charge of everything and everyone. I took great delight in telling God what I wanted and how God should listen to my advice. I felt angry and annoyed when God did not do as I wanted. I would rant and rave, cry and whine, and eat and eat. I was like a child screaming for a sharp knife as this loving and merciful God said, "No – you are not ready to handle a knife." I screamed, "Who are you, God, to tell me what I need." How arrogant and entitled I felt. God loved me enough to allow me to reach a point at which I knew I had a choice between life and death. I asked for life. This meant I had to let God be God.

The gift of abstinence has taught me that I actually knew very little about what was good for me, much less for someone else. I am so grateful that God did not answer my stupid and selfish demands and that God allowed me to see that I can trust God to do God's job. I, in turn, can go forward with strength, hope, and direction toward a happy and useful life.

For today, I trust that God is in control of my life.

Mask of Denial

Halloween is a day to wear a mask and to say "trick or treat." A day to collect and eat candy.

Before FAA recovery, every day was Halloween for me. Every day I wore a mask. I wore a mask when I went shopping for clothes, pretending I liked what was available in my size when really I would purchase anything that fit. I wore a smiling mask while behind the mask I was crying.

Every day I collected and stashed food, lying and denying the horror of my food addiction. I tricked myself into thinking that I was fine and that everyone else was a little crazy. I kept my stash of sugar, flour, and wheat to myself. There was no sharing or caring. I would get cavities from sugar and high cholesterol from fat. And I was in fear of the almighty scale.

This Halloween there will be no tricks and no treats of the sugar variety. Instead, I will treat myself to recovery. Halloween has become a day of gratitude, in which I keep my memory green as to the horrors of my active food addiction.

For today, I treat myself to the good things in life that come from living in abstinence.

Learning Who Is My Higher Power

Sought through prayer and meditation to improve our conscious contact with God, as we understood God, praying only for knowledge of God's will for us, and the power to carry that out. (FAA Step Eleven)

Step Eleven suggests we seek to improve our conscious contact with God, as we understand God. We do this through prayer and meditation. I understand these two words as talking with God and listening. I had very little experience with either of them before I found FAA.

I lived so much of my life from my unconscious, or through my food addiction trying to get unconscious. Living a life of isolation with very few skills in asking for help or in listening to others had become a way of life.

The working of the first ten Steps with my sponsor's guidance helped me to get out of isolation. Abstinence brought consciousness and feelings. Making the decision to turn my will and life over to God's care was a beginning of seeking God's will. Making amends raised my self-esteem to the level of equality with others. The more my life improved, the more I desired a relationship with God.

For today, I keep my prayer and meditation simple. I listen to my heart, knowing that that is where I hear God's voice.

The Journey Unfolds

As we progress in recovery, the path narrows.

As we become more finely attuned to how we are feeling physically, we may find that we need to eliminate certain foods that we could once tolerate.

As we become more finely attuned to how we are feeling emotionally, we may find that we need to make amends promptly. Some of our character defects, once seemingly insignificant, we now recognize as unacceptable.

As we become more finely attuned to how we are feeling spiritually, we develop a keener sense of our need for closer contact with our Higher Power, in whatever way that we define our Higher Power.

The changes that we make as we progress in recovery attest to the lessons that we have learned and the clarity that we have gained.

In early recovery, we need leeway to meander as we adapt to our new life style. Once we find our equilibrium, we can walk a straighter line. We are confident in our direction. We may not know where we are headed, but we find that we are being guided. We are on the right path.

For today, I thank God for gently revealing the right path to me.

Asking for Help

Prayer throughout the day keeps us in conscious contact with our Higher Power. Upon arising, we pray for an abstinent day. At day's close, we thank God for this gift.

During the day, we maintain our dialogue with God. The Serenity Prayer is a simple and soothing mantra that we invoke whenever life frazzles our nerves. We ask for guidance and strength whenever we need it. God is always there for us.

We pause for a moment before each meal to give thanks for our abstinent food and for the gift of recovery. We practice turning over to God that which we cannot control. We ask for help in letting go of attempts to control people, places, and circumstances over which we are powerless.

It is said that *ego* stands for *easing God out.* With God at the center of our day, our ego's desire for control, for addictive foods, and for destruction will neither harm nor torment us. With prayer, our lives grow ever more serene, fulfilling, and joyous.

For today, I keep the line of communication with my Higher Power open and honest.

Nature's Lessons

I tried endlessly and unsuccessfully to meditate. I used all the methods I had heard at meetings or read in books. I tried to feel the silence and presence of my Higher Power, but I would usually drift off to sleep.

One day I collected seeds and took a good look at one of the tiny seeds in my hand. Suddenly, I realized that seed already contained everything that it would be: its color, its odor, its height, whether it preferred shade or sunlight. A deep feeling of serenity and peace overpowered me as I saw the order in the universe. Tears came as I realized that at last I was meditating.

FAA is the soil in which we grow. Meetings are the water that we need to survive. Phone calls and literature are our fertilizers. The sun is our Higher Power. What a miracle!

For today, I strengthen my abstinence by spending time in meditation, trusting that all I need will be revealed to me.

No Hard Sell

Our public relations policy is based on attraction rather than promotion; we need always maintain personal anonymity at the level of press, radio, and films. (FAA Tradition Eleven)

Public relations work in FAA involves providing information to the public in a loving, caring way. Some of the ways in which we do this are by posting notices at a local market, donating an FAA book to a library, and arranging for public service announcements in the local newspaper. We also reach out one to one, guiding other food addicts to our doors with no thought of personal gain.

At the level of press, we accentuate the FAA program and downplay the individual. This is why we must remain anonymous. No one person should represent FAA as a whole. In the media, we do not disclose our full names or allow ourselves to be identified. This assures our audience that anonymity is precious and must be preserved.

Like all our Traditions, Tradition Eleven is grounded in the spirituality of our program. It encourages us to inform the world of our existence without feeding our own egos. Our public relations policy is ongoing. We continue to reach out to the newcomer.

For today, I can reach out to a still-suffering food addict.

Acceptance and Serenity Go Hand in Hand

My serenity is directly proportional to my level of acceptance. Accepting my food addiction was difficult at first, but now it's something for which I am grateful.

Accepting that I may not need to lose any more weight is difficult but relieves me of the obsession with the scale.

Accepting that I can consult with someone in program when making decisions allows me to see God in other people.

Accepting that all I have is today allows me to live in the moment.

As I continue to surrender to my Higher Power, I am learning that acceptance is like removing hundreds of pounds from my shoulders. I have nothing to feel sorry about, nothing to fear, nothing to hate. Acceptance is the key to my serenity today. The more I accept, the more I am able to live my Higher Power's will for me because I am free to listen and to receive the message. When I am not accepting, I am obsessing, and I am not present to receive the gifts in today.

For today, I trust my Higher Power to be in charge of my recovery process.

Abstinence Is My Foundation

I used to see abstinence as a goal. I just needed to get through this day or through a string of days. Then I could continue to tally up my days, weeks, and months of abstinence.

Now I see abstinence as the foundation upon which I build a life. Once the foundation is in place, I can create the rooms I want and the colors I want. I get great joy in finding out what I'm comfortable with and what makes me feel cozy and content. But the foundation must be strong and solid or everything comes crashing down.

Abstinence is my foundation. It can feel uninteresting sometimes, but it supports all of my activities and relationships as well as my connection to my Higher Power. I feel serene. So I pay a lot of attention to that foundation. I take care of it on a daily basis.

For today, I make sure that the foundation of my life is kept clean and strong.

Fellowship

One of the most important things I have learned in FAA is that I cannot recover alone. We need each other in order to recover. Not that we don't have a lot of fun together, but no one joins for a lark.

We need people who love us enough to tell us the truth. We need accurate information on how to treat our disease. We need to see how others develop a relationship with a Higher Power.

We need encouragement when we are stressed and celebration when we are triumphant. We need to follow the example of others who use the tools; who don't pick up sugar, flour, or wheat no matter what; and who persevere through many life events.

We need long-timers to vanquish any doubt that recovery can be lasting and real and to guide us through the Steps. We need newcomers to remind us of the pain of active addiction and the joy of how abstinence transforms lives.

We need each other. What a wonderful gift fellowship is, where we give and receive all that we need for recovery, day by day. In the process, we dry tears and hear the laughter in the rooms.

For today, I pray to remain gratefully aware that together, we are blessed through fellowship.

Honestly Taking Responsibility

Not only can I practice Steps Ten and Eleven on a daily basis, but they can also form the cornerstone of my recovery.

The condensed version of the Eleventh Step is "quiet the mind; open the heart." My knowledge of what is best is based on my perceptions of my tiny world. When I pray in accordance with the Eleventh Step, I am asking to know what thoughts and feelings God wants me to have and pray for the power to translate them into action. It is simple. I reaffirm that God is a power greater than myself. Only God knows what I need. God softly whispers to me all day long.

When I'm doing my Tenth Step inventory, I check to see if I have listened well. If not, where do I need to make amends? The making of amends is beginning to occur more quickly. I love it best when I catch myself before I say or do something that would require an amends. Then no amends are needed!

For today, I can polish the rocks life hands me – turning them into gems.

Changing Friendships

I thought I couldn't do without my old friends – chocolate, peanut butter, ice cream, and baked goods. I turned to them more and more as my food addiction grew. I tried to maintain a relationship with these old friends, telling myself that I could control them, but my disease always called for more and more. No matter how much I consumed, there was never enough. I felt empty inside.

My old friends turned out to be my enemies. They kept me in the bondage of isolation, self-hate, guilt, and ill health. Yet there seemed to be no way to exist without them.

Today, thanks to the program of Food Addicts Anonymous, abstinence is my friend. One day at a time, I experience freedom by surrendering and following my abstinent food plan, working the Steps, calling my sponsor, and writing. I am grateful for the variety of tastes, colors, and textures of healthy foods that nurture my body and soul.

For today, I ask God to help me stick with my true friend – abstinence.

First, We Become Aware

The beginning of recovery from the disease of food addiction is awareness. For many years I accepted being fat. At least I thought I did. I ignored the looks and comments and acted as if everything was fine. I knew everyone smaller than me was thin and everyone larger than me was fat. I finally reached a bottom with my weight as high as it had ever been, my health deteriorating and my absolute inability to stop eating.

When I came to FAA, I saw my life for what it was. That day I admitted that I was powerless over my food addiction and my life was unmanageable. This new acceptance was uncomfortable at first, because it required action – going to meetings, making calls, getting a sponsor, committing my food, working the Steps and dealing with my feelings. Freedom from sugar, flour, and wheat and using the tools of recovery give me so many opportunities now for growth and happiness.

Once I accepted the fact that I am a food addict and was willing to put the work into my recovery, instead of the disease, I found life. I no longer need to look at others or myself as fat or thin. I revere the life I have.

For today, I bask in the rewards of living life in abstinent recovery, making a gratitude list in order to keep myself humble.

The Four S's of Meditation

As part of working the Eleventh Step, I need to meditate to embrace my mind, emotions, and intuition. My soul needs this nourishment of enlightenment. I need my Higher Power's light and strength. This brings out the good in me.

Meditation has four S's: Silence, Surrender, Solitude, and Simplicity.

Silence allows me to hear the messages that my Higher Power has for me.

Surrender has me let go of my troubles so that my Higher Power can take over.

Solitude allows me to give my full attention to my Higher Power.

Simplicity makes it much easier to meditate. Daily meditation strengthens and renews my conscious contact with my Higher Power.

For today, I will take the time to meditate and reflect on my new life.

Roadmap to Recovery

I'm a food addict who requires a roadmap for my recovery. This roadmap is laid out in the FAA program.

I have tried every way I could think of to handle food my way. My Higher Power stood by patiently and waited for me to ask for directions. My Higher Power's way allows for healing on all levels: physical, emotional, and spiritual.

It's not easy to follow this path. However, it is simple. Willingness to change is necessary. My Higher Power is there to help me meet these changes and avoid the roadblocks of relapse. One such change is to reach out and help a fellow food addict. The payoff is that the more I share, the more I have to share.

I like this new road I'm traveling and I share my spiritual journey with fellow recovering food addicts.

For today, I use the FAA roadmap not only to help myself, but also to help another suffering food addict.

Freedom Comes With Planning

I know that living in recovery is so much easier than living in the disease of food addiction. Yet, I struggle some days to do what I have learned. Sometimes I resent planning my food. The disease tells me that normal people don't have to plan their food, but this is simply untrue. People who do not understand food addiction tell me to lighten up. Then, sanity says, everyone has to make decisions about food. Although it may appear that some people can just grab whatever is available, they are probably relying on a plan that they instinctively know.

I can change the way I look at planning my food. I can be grateful that this planning is freeing me from obsessions, reducing the chaos in my life, and giving me the opportunity to love myself. I must remember that I have a life-threatening disease. I am worth the effort of planning my food to nourish my body. I enhance my emotional and spiritual life by applying the Steps.

For today, I acknowledge that abstinence is the highest form of self-love.

Practicing the Eleventh Step

Sought through prayer and meditation to improve our conscious contact with God, as we understood God, praying only for knowledge of God's will for us and the power to carry that out. (FAA Step Eleven)

- Today I ask for help in staying in the present.

- Today I ask for help in turning my attention toward helping others.

- Today I fill myself with good thoughts and good deeds.

- Today I surround myself with positive people.

- Today I choose to nourish my body with the healthy foods available on the food plan.

- Today I focus on improving my conscious contact with my Higher Power. I pray for the wisdom to be open to hear what I need to hear from the people carrying God's message.

For today, I fill myself up by listening to God and listening to the wisdom that God sends me through others.

Reach Out and Phone Someone

The phone is a great tool for staying connected to other food addicts, building relationships in recovery, and getting support when I am struggling. When I have a problem, I know that I can pick up the phone and talk about it with another recovering food addict. And by exercising this tool, I build a network of friends.

Sometimes I feel nervous calling someone I don't know well, but usually I am pleasantly surprised by how caring, supportive, and helpful that person is. Calling a newcomer or a fellow food addict who is struggling is a form of service, and service keeps me abstinent.

The fellowship of FAA sustains me when my attitude stumbles. The FAA literature reminds me that we are all recovering from food addiction together. I can't do this alone. I now want others to be part of my recovery journey.

For today, I ask my Higher Power for the courage to make a few phone calls, a form of love and service at my fingertips 24 hours a day.

Feeling Feelings

With the gift of abstinence comes the gift of feelings. Some of these feelings are elixirs for the soul – joy, happiness, contentment, love. Some of these feelings are raw, abrasive, and very painful. Life is a mixture of all of these feelings. Most of us are blessed with the good ones at least part of the time, but none of us can escape the bad ones.

In abstinence, I feel my feelings, the good and the bad. The gift of abstinence is that I handle bad feelings without numbing them by bingeing on sugar, flour, or wheat. Numbing painful feelings does not make them go away. Nor does it resolve a painful situation. In fact, it magnifies the pain.

No problem is so bad that one bite of binge food won't make it worse. Only with abstinence, can I appreciate the good feelings, and plow through the bad. Only with abstinence, can I handle life on life's terms and come out on the other side with peace, dignity, and self-respect. When pain erupts in my life, I stop doing whatever is causing it and start doing whatever it takes to eliminate it.

For today, I choose abstinence. I will feel all my feelings, process them, and handle them with help from my Higher Power.

Being Grateful for Being a Food Addict

When I first heard a fellow FAA member say, "I'm a very grateful food addict," I thought they were crazy. I had suffered years of unsuccessful dieting and a lack of control around addictive food. Whatever could anyone possibly be grateful for concerning food addiction?

Once I became abstinent, I experienced life in ways beyond imagination. My cravings began to disappear, and healthy foods actually taste better. I am grateful that I actually enjoy food more and eat a variety of foods I would have never discovered had it not been for the FAA food plan.

Life takes on new dimensions when we are abstinent. We have clarity. For the first time, we are able to gain control over our impulses, as long as we appeal to our Higher Power. Our bodies begin to heal and physical ailments that have plagued us for years sometimes disappear. As the physical recovery progresses and we head toward our ideal weight, shopping for clothes becomes fun rather than a chore.

What we have given up is minuscule compared to what we have gained in abstinence.

For today, I appreciate the gifts I receive from abstinence rather than concentrate on what I am supposedly missing.

Replacing Old Habits

A wise and famous teacher once stated that it was impossible to change a habit. You could only replace a habit with another one that was so much more preferable that you would choose it over and over again.

Those FAA members who have been able to maintain long-term abstinence have experienced this, and love the difference that abstinence from sugar, flour, and wheat has brought to their lives.

Free from cravings, abstinence becomes easier and easier to choose. Old habits are replaced with ones that support abstinence. Weighing and measuring, which may have been so difficult to do while eating addictive foods, becomes easier.

It was tragic that this wise teacher had an abrupt ending to his own life from medical complications attributable to food addiction. We are fortunate to have a program that offers us a solution.

For today, let me always remember that all the wisdom in the world won't change the fact that I am a food addict.

Using Technology to Stay Abstinent

I spent years trying all of the latest gadgets to obtain a normal weight, including digital treadmills, juicers, calorie counters, carbohydrate counters, the newest cookware, and computer programs to track my intake and output. But the latest technology could not address the fact that I am addicted to sugar, flour, and wheat. I still hoped, however, that the right gadget would come along that would free me from my prison of addiction.

Indeed, technology can help me stay abstinent. Online meetings, phone meetings, the FAA loop, e-mails, CDs, DVDs, and cell phones aid me in staying connected with the fellowship of FAA. Many times simply reaching out to another member keeps me abstinent.

My recovery is most dependent on getting on my knees and asking for help from my Higher Power. No state-of-the-art technology is required.

For today, I pray to discern the difference between technology that leads me into denial of my disease and technology that supports my abstinence.

Listening To My Higher Power

Along with following a plan of sound nutrition, FAA emphasizes the importance of working the Twelve Steps. God speaks to each of us throughout the day and working Step Eleven is a formal method. Perhaps when we first tried to do Step Eleven we purchased every meditation book we could find to teach us how to meditate perfectly.

We may have heard that talking to our Higher Power is praying and that meditation is listening. We may have also heard about "keeping it simple." Prayer can be as simple as "Help me." Meditation can be as simple as sitting quietly for five minutes. We can just sit, listen, and do nothing else. We can ask God to fill us with gratitude, love, and peace.

After years of abstinence, I occasionally ask myself: "Can it be this simple?" Our problems find solutions. Our prayers are answered. We can be witnesses to the healing taking place within. What we give back are our stories and our love.

For today, I seek to show love to others and myself.

Clarity Brings Appreciation

As our days of abstinence increase, our head clears and we are able to stay in the present moment. Our lives become open to good things. We begin to see and appreciate our blessings, and our appreciation brings more good things our way. We take the time to find joy in everyday occurrences – the way the sun glimmers through the leaves, the exuberance of children as they run by, the coolness of the autumn air on our skin, the note that we get from a friend, a favorite book or magazine that we now have time to read.

Staying in the present strengthens our appreciation and our recovery. Everyday events become holy. We can watch a sunset without thinking, "What will I binge on next?" or "How much do I weigh?" Our minds no longer wander – at least, not very far or for very long. We now have the freedom to live the life that we were meant to live.

Where food was once the center of our lives, we now choose recovery and are able to dream bigger and work harder at making our dreams come true.

For today, I seek out things to appreciate in my life in this moment.

Doing What We Can

There are days when I use all the tools: attend a meeting, make phone calls, read, write, call my sponsor, have sponsees call me. Then there are days when I get too busy, am too much into my own thoughts, or am unwilling to take the time to do what I know I need to do to stay healthy.

Balking at my recovery is a dangerous attitude if left unattended for too long. I can accept that some days I will have more energy and some days I will have less energy, but I pray that I will always have the energy to ask my Higher Power for the willingness to be abstinent. No matter what, I weigh and measure my food and stay away from sugar, flour, and wheat.

It is during the times that I am least willing that I need to grab the tools more than ever. If I pray for the willingness, I have already taken the most important step of surrendering my will.

For today, I ask God for the willingness to be abstinent no matter what.

Joy of Balance

Sometimes the highlight of our day is connecting with fellow food addicts on the phone or at meetings. We may enjoy this exhilarating feeling. It may even replace a similar feeling that we may have experienced when anticipating a binge. It is a good feeling to share our joys, pain, and life in general with someone who can relate. That is the beauty of the fellowship. If we use the tools to connect with other people, our world broadens and our days are brighter.

Sometimes, rather than talking to others, we find that quiet reflection is what is needed. We may read and write or be still and listen.

We need both experiences – communication with others and communication with ourselves – to keep us in balance. We trust that our Higher Power will show us what is good for us on any given day.

For today, I remember my real source of peace and strength and listen for guidance.

I Am a Food Addict

I can't afford for one minute to forget that I'm a food addict. The minute I forget is when the disease gets stronger than ever. To forget that I am a food addict is to be deluded into believing that I can be like other people when it comes to food. I begin to believe that I am like people who can take just one piece of cake or who eat only when they are hungry.

If I listen to the voice of recovery, I accept that my brain chemistry differs from that of non-food addicts. Those who are not addicted to sugar, flour, and wheat do not process their everyday experiences by bingeing or purging. I will never be one of those people. I must always remember that my brain chemistry is such that my addictive substances affect my body, my mind, and my spirit, which is why food addiction is thought of as a threefold disease.

I am a food addict who needs the boundaries of the food plan, the Twelve Steps, and the Twelve Traditions. I can't work this program of recovery by myself, even though I've tried. I need the fellowship of other food addicts who think and feel as I do. We feed each other's spirits instead of feeding the disease.

For today, I remember that the disease and my recovery are threefold.

It's a Priority

For some of us, prayer is a new concept. Others of us have prayed all of our lives but never practiced the spiritual discipline of meditation.

Prayer is simply talking to my Higher Power. I ask my Higher Power for what I need, trusting my Higher Power knows what's best for me, because I've turned my will over to my Higher Power's care in Step Three. I've learned to pray for me, not just others, and for God to change me, not everybody else.

Meditation can be defined as slowing down long enough to hear God. My disease does not want me to do this. It wants me to fill up my life, so I don't have room left in my schedule for quiet time with my Higher Power. Why? Because conscious contact with my Higher Power gives me the power to carry out his will for me – abstinence, continued recovery, and carrying the message to the food addict who is still suffering.

For today, I make it my priority to spend quiet time through prayer and meditation to improve my conscious contact with God.

A Tool for Serenity and Peace

The Steps to Recovery book states, as part of our decision in Step Three, to "turn our will and our lives over to the care of God as we understood God." We can begin by praying the Serenity Prayer as part of our daily living. Spending time with our Higher Power in writing an extended version of this prayer is a way to get through those situations that could lead us back to our addictive substances. Here's one example:

God [my Higher Power], grant me the serenity [a quiet calm and peace that is a gift from you] to accept the things I cannot change [that I am a food addict and that life isn't always fair], courage to change the things I can [my attitude], and the wisdom to know the difference [what is within my power and what is not]. Help me to live my life one day at a time.

Keep me ever mindful that recovery and healing happen one day at a time. Keep me focused on what I need today to stay abstinent and close to you – today and today only. I need your strength to not live in yesterday or tomorrow.

For today, I begin to turn my will and life over to God's care by praying and applying the Serenity Prayer.

A Sponsor's Wisdom

My first FAA sponsor lovingly helped me to learn the program of abstinent eating and living a surrendered life. I would call her in the morning and tell her how I was sure I could not live another day in the sadness of depression. She told me to pray, to stay abstinent, to make my calls, to get to my meeting, and I would be fine.

"Oh no," I raged. "It is not that easy. You don't understand. I am really hurting here."

Quietly, she said, "Pray, stay abstinent, make your calls, get to your meetings, and maybe write a little about this."

I told her that I wanted to call her and have her take all my pain away. She laughed! She said that God would take the pain away as I followed the program. And you know what? God did.

For today, I remember how sick I was and how much progress I have made with the help of my sponsor.

Waiting for a Reply

In this electronic age, many of us correspond by e-mail. If we e-mail a question and don't get a response immediately, we may get anxious and shut down the computer. We never get to know the recipient's response.

Perhaps this is true of God as well. If we go to God in prayer asking for help and we do not wait in meditation for an answer, we may delete our question before the answer is received.

When we sit in meditation, we realize that answers do not always come immediately but they do come. We can listen for that small voice within us.

For today, I wait for a clear answer to my prayer. I am willing to clear my mind of the need for a fix and wait patiently.

Making the Important Connection

Prayer is speaking to God. Meditation is being still and listening to God. Combining our speaking and listening to our Higher Power creates a humble, joyous and peaceful existence. We may find meditation difficult. Food addicts are not used to sitting still and experiencing quiet, empty space. We might also sense that we have not a moment to spare, now that we finally have the energy and clarity of abstinence.

Meditation is one of the keys to stable long-term abstinence. Connecting with our Higher Power is a priority. The willingness to sit still for five, ten, or twenty minutes helps us develop a fundamental serenity and connection with our Higher Power, without which we remain ever vulnerable to breaking our abstinence.

For today, I surrender to quiet time to deepen my connection with a loving God.

Spiritual Goal

Having had a spiritual awakening as the result of these steps, we tried to carry this message to food addicts, and to practice these principles in all our affairs.
(FAA Step Twelve)

To be awakened spiritually is the goal of the Twelve Step program. It is to find that life force living within, that divine spark that touches our human emotions so we may live among others in a free state of mind and body without sugar, flour, and wheat or extra food.

To fully understand this Step, I have to imagine what the word awaken means. When I first wake up in the morning, I have yet to become fully conscious. There are certain routines that I practice to help me become more awake. As the day progresses, I am better in tune with the universe.

So it is with my awakening spirituality. If I want to keep what I have, then I must work the Steps and pass what I have learned on to others. I grow in my recovery when I practice these principles with newcomers, longtimers, and people who have not heard of the Twelve Step program. As I carry out God's will, I become pleasing to my Higher Power.

For today, I ask God to help me carry the message of the Twelve Step way of life and the FAA program.

Claiming My Seat

Each time I attend a phone meeting, I hear people claiming their seat: owning up to the fact that they are food addicts. They have relinquished the addictive destructive substances and behaviors that had gotten them into trouble.

I claim my seat today. I no longer want the substances and behaviors that were literally killing me before recovery. My seat is right here, in the lap of recovery and in the lap of the God of my understanding. By the grace of God, my seat is not getting bigger. I already hit my bottom. It can only get better from here.

For today, I will remain in the seat of recovery. It's a lot better than standing in the quicksand of the disease!

Twelve-Step Wings

There are twists and turns in life which challenge our faith and ultimately chip away at our spirituality. They may give us good cause to take control one more time. These could be major events such as open-heart surgery or simpler events like making a decision to adjust our food plan. We may find ourselves asking, "Why me?"

It may be hard to remember that we now have a place to discuss how we feel. By sharing what is on our mind with other recovering people, the power that our problems holds diminish, and our faith blossoms. With the surge of faith comes a sweet surrender to our Higher Power.

With God and faith in our lives, we are able to pray for God's message and stay quiet. The message comes swiftly, uncertainty is removed, and soon we are out of the pain. The dilemma becomes clear. Once we see a clear path, we can take the actions that are productive, because we are no longer impeded by worry.

Productive gathering of facts, sharing the dilemma with other FAA members, absolute surrender to a Higher Power, and productive actions give us the experience, strength, and hope to walk through any twists and turns. Our lives are then placed on a higher plane of living and we have more to give in our Twelve-Step work.

For today, I welcome risks and challenges.

A Spiritual Awakening

When we first embark on the path of the Twelve Steps in FAA, we don't know where it will lead us. But we start because we are desperate to end the pain and hopelessness that we are living in.

As we proceed on our journey through each Step, we see that we need not stay stuck in the misery of food addiction. If we faithfully put each Step into effect in our lives, we will discover we have had an awakening of our spirit. We have been put in touch with something beyond ourselves, recognizing a Higher Power to whom we can turn.

The best way to keep this newfound energy is to carry the FAA message of hope and love to others. It has been proven repeatedly that in giving it away we keep our own recovery. Each newcomer whom we see at a meeting offers us an opportunity to strengthen our own understanding and demonstrate our gratitude. As we comfort others, we inspire their trust in the fellowship.

As we continue to apply the principles that we learn from working the Steps, we renew our spiritual connection. We reinforce the hope, strength, self-confidence, and spiritual awareness that the Steps give us.

For today, I practice these principles in all my affairs.

Carrying the Message

Addiction fragmented our lives, our personalities, and our souls. Through recovery, these shattered pieces are gently placed back together, the stronger for having been broken. We become whole and blessed with a deep understanding and appreciation of this new harmony in our lives. We have attained a higher state of consciousness, a spiritual awakening.

We have much to give. We carry the message by doing service within the fellowship, and sharing our recovery with those outside of the fellowship when appropriate. Our spiritual awakening by its nature permeates every aspect of our lives. We conduct our lives with integrity. We are honest in our business affairs, we seek harmony in family life, and treat ourselves, and all those with whom we have contact each day, with acceptance, compassion, and respect.

With vigilant practice, living life from a spiritual perspective becomes second nature. Old issues will rise again, and we will face new challenges. We respond from a secure emotional center – with our trust in God. The struggle has passed. We have found serenity.

For today, I ask for guidance from my Higher Power as I seek to practice these principles in all my affairs.

Moving Towards Self-Love

Food had always been comfort and love for me. Rather than using food to fuel my body, I used it to help me celebrate successes and mourn losses. After all, what was a party without food? How could I face disappointment without sweets?

Food is a drug for me. It helps me bury my feelings. I have yet to find a therapist or an exercise program that cures food addiction.

My Higher Power, speaking through others, does for me what I cannot do for myself. With abstinence and working the Twelve Steps of FAA, I can love and take care of myself. I deserve it and need it. I now understand that I had to have a lot of self-hatred to treat my body the way I did. I can forgive myself for what I inflicted on my body. I was a victim of my disease. What I needed was love and nurturing. And one day at a time in FAA, that is exactly what I get.

My body is a gift from my Higher Power, and I will treat it with the care it deserves.

For today, I see my value and give myself love and nurturing through the choices I make.

Gratitude in Action

Having had a spiritual awakening as the result of these steps, we tried to carry this message to other food addicts and to practice these principles in all our affairs. (FAA Step Twelve)

Gratitude is Step Twelve in action. In practicing the Twelfth Step, we share with others our experience before coming to FAA and then what we have received.

We are given much by our sponsors, including their valuable time. We begin to think and see things clearly. In working the Steps, we are fully awake – not half-awake, like we used to be. This awakening is not an overnight event, but a gradual process.

We may be hesitant to sponsor a newcomer. However, if we have one more day than that person does, we have something to give away. Through our sharing and caring, we maintain our serenity.

We carry the message to give away what we have, so that we may in turn keep it. We hope that the newcomer stays abstinent, but, regardless, we will remain abstinent. Our gratitude knows no bounds.

For today, I am grateful that I have the ability to give to others through sponsorship.

Freedom From Perfectionism

I used to strive to be the best at everything. I wanted unlimited admiration and validation. I had to be the thinnest, the prettiest, the smartest, and the most successful. Otherwise, I was nothing.

Of course, any success was never enough. Food helped to quell my continual frustration of not achieving perfection and fed the fantasy that my ambitions were indeed attainable. Let me binge and pass out, and tomorrow I will try a little harder.

In recovery I am learning to trust that God has a plan for me. I can relax; I am striving for progress not perfection. Today I seek to embrace new values: the clarity of thought that abstinence gives; the love and compassion that I give and receive each day; and the joy of reaching out to help others, especially fellow food addicts.

I no longer strive to be the best. If I slowly grow wiser, kinder, and happier over time, then I am a success.

For today, I ask God to keep me spiritually centered so that I may fully experience the joy of growing in wisdom and compassion.

The Power of We

"We cannot do it alone." (<u>Food Addicts Anonymous,</u> *Some Thoughts on Spirituality*)

As I begin the day, I think about all the recovering food addicts in different parts of the world who are a part of my family. To know that I never again have to be alone in this disease is a comfort. It also gives me the ability to stay abstinent today and to strengthen my relationships.

I reach out to other members of FAA, both newcomers and old-timers. I am always amazed to find that I am not alone in my diseased thoughts. I am not the only one who did weird things with and around food. The shame I feel lessens, and another ray of hope of recovery shines on me.

Whether I see FAA members at a meeting, talk with them on the phone, or share with them online, I know that I can depend on them for support and love. Trying to recover alone is difficult. But with other food addicts to share with, I can stay on the path of physical, mental, and spiritual recovery.

For today, I am grateful that I am not alone in my recovery.

Stay Plugged In

When I was thinking about avoiding relapse around the holidays, I thought about my Christmas tree and the electrical outlet that we use to illuminate the room with the magnificent lights. Without that connection, we'd be sitting in the dark. Well, that outlet has two open slots.

If I put up too many lights or get too involved with decorating or shopping or planning activities, both outlets get used and there is no place for me to make the connection to my source of energy. My Higher Power (energy) is snuffed out (dark). I need to keep my inner light burning! I need to stay plugged in! I need to do a Tenth Step inventory throughout the day to keep my mind refreshed and renewed.

For today, I am not too busy to plug into the source and strength provided by my Higher Power.

No Matter What

Although we cannot depend on willpower alone to maintain abstinence, its intermittent use is essential. It certainly takes some willpower to move through the stormy sea of detoxification, when cravings are fierce. But we soon learn that rather than fight temptation, we can hand it over to our Higher Power. Eventually we reach calmer waters.

The stronger our recovery, the less need there is to resort to willpower. However, it takes time to develop serenity and new coping skills, because storms will routinely rock our boat. When tempted to return to that old tried and true pain reliever – addictive foods, we can invoke the mantra, "Remain abstinent, no matter what."

For most food addicts, willpower can take us only so far. By surrendering to a power greater than ourselves, we find that we can weather the cravings and allow the storm to pass. Surprisingly, the wait is usually short – sometimes as short as 20 minutes. And we often find that the more violent the storm, the swifter its passing.

When the clouds finally blow over, we can greet the sun with a clear mind and a healthy body.

For today, I trust that my Higher Power will not give me more than I can bear, as I sail through tempests on this journey.

Witnessing the Promises

The FAA promises do not manifest suddenly in our lives. From the very moment we begin our journey of recovery we catch glimpses and glimmers, which grow ever brighter as we continue on our way.

The basic themes behind the promises are that we will let go of paralyzing fear, doubt, and self-obsession and that we become present, alert, optimistic, and happy. As these changes occur, we grow ever more willing and able to meet life on life's terms. And our lives respond to this acknowledgment and attention by blossoming fully.

The brilliance of the promises is that we become fully aware of them in our lives. After all, life can be quite wonderful, but not if we fail to take note of the blessings around us.

We are promised not just a good life, but also the gift of perceiving the full glory of this good life.

For today, I thank God for the gift of clearly perceiving the wonderful changes recovery brings to my life and for the inspiration and joy that such awareness bestows.

Our Job and Purpose

When we look at Step Twelve, "Having had a spiritual awakening as the result of these Steps, we tried to carry this message to food addicts and to practice these principles in all our affairs," we know that carrying the message is our job. Each member of FAA is responsible for reaching out to newcomers. We welcome newcomers, answer their questions, and encourage them to come back. We are the ones best qualified to do this. We are food addicts in recovery. We share, and we encourage newcomers to share. We know that healing begins here.

Even if in our outside lives we carry expert titles such as therapist or doctor, when we attend an FAA meeting we are all equal. We have no authority figures. We share only our experience, strength, and hope, one recovering food addict to another.

For today, I reach out my hand to help another suffering food addict.

The Growth Choice

With abstinence, my thoughts today are not mired in when, where, and how I'll get my binge foods. Instead, I can turn my thoughts to living life on life's terms.

Before FAA, I had a huge problem with acceptance. I have since learned that my life is mine to create: I no longer allow other people to dictate my life to me.

We grow or we go. I choose to grow. With the endless knowledge and ongoing support available in this program, I can design my plan for living. Further, as I go about creating my life the way I want to live it, I value the importance of abstinence.

If I do not commit myself to abstinence, then all of my choices are made for me. My world crumbles into little fragments, and I wind up living on other people's terms.

Today I look forward to my simple food plan that allows me to be abstinent. I have no desire to eat food that is not on my plan. If I am given binge foods as a gift, I can donate them to an organization that cares for people in need. This gives me an opportunity to give back and to make living amends.

For today, I focus on the life I have because of abstinence and of living the FAA program of recovery.

Acceptance is the Answer

To get to a place of acceptance and surrender, you told me I first had to accept myself exactly as I was. I needed to begin loving myself enough to want to change. I had to become teachable and then I had to accept help.

I had a spiritual awakening when I realized that it really is all about me – all of it. No one is supposed to, has to, wants to, or is able to fix me. I was sure that there was some magic that could fix me so that one day I would wake up and not want to eat the whole pound of candy.

The magic turned out to be the healing power of FAA. Today when I see a bag of candy, it no longer calls my name. It doesn't recognize me and I don't want it. The cravings are gone.

It is only with gut-level acceptance that I am able to take the next right action that is necessary. Today I am a food addict. Today I have a plan from which I don't deviate. I have a daily reprieve.

For today, I accept and love myself. I am able to take responsibility for my own recovery.

It's all in a Day's Work

As I start this day at work, I may be confronted by foods that are brought in by my fellow workers. This day I will exercise my choice to say no to the smorgasbord of donuts, bagels, and pastries and to say yes to my recovery. For today my choice is to be healthy and abstinent.

When the disease of food addiction speaks loudly and screams in my face to join in and just have a little, I can walk into the restroom and pray. I can pick up the phone and call another food addict or my sponsor. I can walk out for a breath of fresh air to regain my composure and renew my commitment to an abstinent day.

I know that by staying abstinent through each trying circumstance, one day at a time, my desire to be well and to be true to myself will be strengthened. For today, I gratefully start the workday abstinently, and when my head hits the pillow at night, I thank my Higher Power for another day of abstinence.

For today, I am grateful that this fellowship shows me that I can have a wonderful life without succumbing to addictive foods.

Moderation and Balance

Moderation and balance are essential to our recovery. In active addiction, we created and experienced a world of extremes – all or nothing. We engaged in extreme eating and exercise. Our weight was rarely stable. Our emotions swung from giddy highs to devastating lows. Sleep may have been irregular. Our sex lives may have been repressed or irresponsible. Financial security was often unpredictable. Relationships were either on or off.

Our addictive behavior was the only real constant. It provided a certain frame of reference. No matter how erratic our lives became, we always had our substance for comfort. It created an illusion of stability as the swirl of madness around us continued. Now we have lost this illusion. Chaos without our numbing substance is unsustainable. To maintain our recovery, we need real stability in our lives to replace the illusion.

The principles of moderation and balance guide us. Our food plan provides moderate, balanced eating. We then bring this moderation and balance to other areas of our life: sleep, work, finances, and relationships. With our lives in order, we are free to grow emotionally and spiritually.

For today, I ask God to help me practice moderation in all things, so that I may live a harmonious, balanced life.

Help Always Comes

I had been abstinent a year when I woke up so irritable I could not stand to be with myself. I was filled with resentment, criticism, and complaints about everyone and everything. With great indignation, I sat in my prayer chair and told God, "I need help and I am not getting out of this chair until you help me. I do not want to break my abstinence. Help me God."

I reviewed what I had learned from my sponsor and my home group. They taught me that feelings are not facts and that I could use the tools to help me deal with my feelings without eating more than I had committed for the day. I knew at my core that eating addictive foods would only make my life worse.

Within a few minutes, I received a call from an FAA member who said that he was thinking of me. I opened my e-mail and found many messages related to handling feelings while remaining abstinent. I called in to a phone meeting, and the topic was that feelings are not facts. OK – I got the message. God was sending me the help that I had asked for.

After several more calls, I could not do anything other than laugh at how alone and grumpy I had felt. I was filled with gratitude and joy. I knew God was taking care of me through the love of people in the program and I had experienced a day of miracles.

For today, I ask God for help and then trust that I'll receive the help I need exactly when I need it.

The Gift of Surrender

Some of us hit dramatic lows in addiction, losing our health and the ability to function in our daily life. Our desperation led us to surrender.

Others of us had a less dramatic story. We were not overweight or underweight, but still we were addicted to food. We were able to show up, maintain appearances, and get by. But we grew sick and tired of being sick and tired. Our drudgery led us to surrender.

Years of the zero-one step dance, that is, on-and-off abstinence finally convinced us that although perhaps we could survive this way indefinitely, life certainly was not getting any better. We realized from witnessing the recovery of fellow food addicts that we did not have to accept a life of frustration, depression, and making do. There was another way. A better life awaited our surrender, so we let go, one day at a time.

Sometimes surrender does not require desperation. Drudgery, though not as dramatic, can eventually wear us down. No matter, we are grateful for anything that has led us to this program. If we surrender, we can look upon our desperation and drudgery as having led us to God and, ultimately, of setting us free.

For today, I thank God for letting me turn my misery into surrender.

Releasing Resentment

We sometimes encounter normal eaters indulging in a sugary item. We may marvel at how these folks can eat just one, not the whole bag, box, or cake. We wonder how they can eat sugary substances without violently scarfing them down, crumbs flying all about, eyes rolling skyward.

So how do normal eaters do it? Well, such people do not have a biochemical sensitivity to sugar! For them, sugar is not a drug. A dose of sugar registers in the non-addict's brain as a little feather tickle, a pleasant sensation, but not a source of extreme stimulation igniting cravings, obsession, and compulsion.

With this knowledge we can release any resentment or envy we have of people who are not food addicts. It is not unfair that such folks can enjoy sugar, flour, and wheat because they do not enjoy these substances as a food addict does. For a food addict, consuming addictive foods is not eating; it is drugging.

In abstinence, we are not deprived of delicious food. In fact, we are introduced to the pleasures of eating in a healthy, nourishing way. With abstinence, we experience the pleasure of different tastes and the sense of satisfaction at the end of a meal.

For today, I thank God for the simple pleasure of eating abstinently.

The Big Picture

Anonymity is the spiritual foundation of all our Traditions, ever reminding us to place principles before personalities. (FAA Tradition Twelve)

We uphold the first part of this Tradition at every meeting, when the leader says, "What you see and hear here – stays here." This anonymity assures safety for our members. We can share without reservation knowing our comments are kept in the confines of the meeting.

It's the second part of this Tradition that brings up character defects. Whenever food addicts walking the recovery path are together, there are many different opinions. We come from different backgrounds, customs, and beliefs. When I was new in FAA and a group decision didn't go my way, I would get resentful and angry. Today, I remind myself to place the principles of the program before the personalities of the fellowship.

It is the obligation of all FAA members to practice the Twelve Traditions as well as the Twelve Steps. Without the constant wisdom of the Traditions to guide us as a fellowship, we may falter and lose our balance.

For today, I apply FAA principles before personalities.

Recognizing Feelings

For most of my life, I never knew that I was stuffing my feelings with food. I just ate most of the time, so I never had the opportunity to feel anything. How sad. I ate to numb the bad feelings and I ended up blocking the good feelings too. Many joys were, at the very least, minimized because I was preoccupied with food or was in a food hangover. On the other hand, blocking feelings protected me from feelings that could have triggered unacceptable and perhaps destructive behaviors.

In abstinence, I have the opportunity to recognize what I am feeling. Sometimes the feelings are painful. I have found ways to name, claim, understand, and cope with all kinds of feelings. Feeling all of my feelings helps me to move forward in my recovery. I can heal once I can acknowledge and manage my feelings. I can allow this healing to flow into relationships and situations in my life.

With abstinence, I have the gift of clarity so that I can make healthy choices instead of acting out or eating in an unhealthy manner.

For today, I remember that what I can feel I can heal.

Healing Through Recovery

"Abstinence will open the door, and by working the Twelve Steps we can recover, one day at a time."
(<u>Food Addicts Anonymous</u>, *Who is a Food Addict?*)

The unknown represents danger – the threat of not being in control, safe and secure in the familiarity of experience. My life as a food addict was defined by fear as well as by anger and resentments. It was easier to suffer the familiar pain, shame, and self-hate than to risk free-falling into some unknown shadowy space, fearful of ending in a total collapse. That was before the pain finally overwhelmed my ability to endure it and became greater than my fear of the unknown.

Growing in faith and trust in a Higher Power and in the support and guidance of FAA and other food addicts, we begin to grow in self-discovery, acceptance, responsibility, and accountability – usually in the most unexpected ways. When we take the action that the principles of the Twelve Steps suggest, our spirits heal.

Despite the uncertainty, I feel peaceful. I seek peace when faced with unfamiliar or unpleasant situations. I am learning to believe in and trust my Higher Power's wisdom that there is some greater good waiting for me, regardless of the fear, anger, or resentment I may feel.

For today, I welcome the gifts that heal my spirit, and I am grateful.

A Circle of Hope

Many of us started out as calm, peaceful people, drawn to quiet endeavors and simplicity. Somewhere along the way, we succumbed to our food addiction, and chaos dominated our lives. The frenzy of getting the food, eating the food, and then working off the food filled our days.

We had to get to the point where we had had enough. We could not continue to dig ourselves into a deeper, darker hole each day. We did not want to be buried alive. However, we had to get to that point of surrender in our own time.

Enter FAA and a healthy way of eating and living. As we began the food plan and working the Twelve Steps, the frenzy abated. We were able to awake each day with a clear mind. Our racing thoughts were slowed; our mind became quiet. Once more, we became peaceful and calm.We have come full circle. We have found ourselves.

For today, I thank God for the simple joy of being myself.

The Easier, Softer Way

"Total abstinence is far easier than perfect moderation." St. Augustine (354-430 C.E.)

This is a day and season in which many of us have memories of sugary treats, floured pastries, overeating, and overindulgence. It is a day when our disease could say, "It would be good to celebrate with just one bite" or "You shouldn't have to weigh and measure today".

As food addicts our disease tells us that just one bite won't *really* make a difference. But often we hear how one bite led to many days, many months, and sometimes years of eating addictively.

We have a freedom with abstinence that cannot be duplicated by addictive eating. Abstinence brings us so much more ability to experience the pleasures in life and the appreciation of those close to us. Abstinence is a serene state of life in which we can hear more clearly what our Higher Power wants for us. So for this day, let us remember the words of wisdom from St. Augustine. If total abstinence is easier than moderation for saints, it is certainly easier for us.

For today, I remember how much easier it is to stay abstinent than to get abstinent. I will celebrate this day by enjoying the company of family and friends.

Surrendering the Sword of Addiction

We food addicts are a strong, tenacious, disciplined, courageous group. We know how to direct our energies and persevere until we reach a goal. Nonetheless, when our efforts are directed at controlling this disease, we find that we have met our match.

Our addiction is like a virus that turns the body against itself. It uses our body's sensitive chemistry to induce cravings, our strength of will to tighten its grip, our independence to keep us isolated, and our intellect to rationalize its hold on us. We will always lose against this disease, because we cannot conquer ourselves.

But we do surrender in FAA. We pass the sword on to our Higher Power. Recovery is not difficult; it flows naturally from abstaining from addictive foods and working the program. Seldom are we tempted to take back the sword and continue the hopeless battle.

When we step out of our own way, the process works. Our role each day is not to fight this disease, but rather to continue those actions that keep us open to surrender: abstinence, prayer, meditation, Step work, fellowship, and practicing the principles in all our affairs.

For today, I surrender the sword of addiction.

Healthy Action

For my entire career as a food addict, I tried everything that I heard about or could dream of to make myself get thin and stay thin! I had a distorted body image. Thinness was all that mattered. Not eating healthy, not recovering from compulsion and addiction, not a sane and manageable life.

It finally dawned on me that I was trying to treat the symptom rather than the disease! Now I have the full picture. I am a food addict. My body and brain cannot handle sugar, flour, or wheat. Only in FAA have I found the solution to my problem.

I have experienced joyful abstinence and relief from the cravings and insanity that had always defeated me. In working the Twelve Steps, I have learned that I must be totally honest, humble, and willing to go to any lengths. FAA is a program of action, and I take action to focus on the solution rather than on the problem.

I absolutely must go to any lengths to stay abstinent. This is the foundation of my recovery. I have learned that the tiniest amount of hidden sugar, flour, or wheat is toxic to me, triggering my addictive brain to yearn, crave, and manipulate me into relapse. If my sponsor and other recovering food addicts tell me that something works for them, then I am willing to incorporate it into my tool chest.

For today, I am constructing a daily life in recovery.

Think, Think, Think

I once was afraid of thinking of food – especially foods not in my best interest. I thought it meant I was not clean enough or that if I really had recovery these thoughts would not occur. More powerful than thoughts was an urge or craving. The truth is that urges and cravings pass. Today I know thoughts are simply thoughts.

There are many ways to change negative thoughts. Some say direct your thoughts and in turn, you can change your feelings. Others suggest we stay quiet and watch the meaning that we assign to a thought. Others think the safest bet is to act our way into better thinking. You can't pray and think at the same time – interrupt your stinking thinking with prayer. Take repetitive thoughts to a meeting, or share with a sponsor. If in doubt, I will leave it out until I can seek guidance of another abstinent person.

For today, I choose not to act on my stinking thinking and I replace my negative thoughts with prayer.

The Multiplier Effect

If I eat over a problem, I then have two problems: the original problem plus the problem of having picked up my addictive substance. There is a third problem as well. In failing to take real action to address the original problem, I let it grow worse. Whether it is unresolved feelings, tasks left undone, or confrontations avoided, these issues are not simply on hold.

If a small kitchen fire flared and I chose to ignore the flames rather than douse them, I would soon have many more problems. I'd have a raging fire wreaking havoc.

Our less compelling problems are the same way. The feelings ignored and repressed by turning to food only grow stronger and may even take a toll on our physical health. The confrontation avoided escalates the unresolved tension between parties. The house becomes messier. Life's problems multiply when we are in active addiction.

For today, I pray to stay abstinent so that my problems and life remain manageable.

Lifting the Veil of Denial

The longer I stay abstinent, the more I realize just how powerless I am over this addiction. Looking back on my life I can see plenty of times where I was out of control with food long before I noted it as a problem. I didn't realize how food was interfering with family time, friendships, and social events. I just wasn't ready.

God opened my eyes to my unmanageable behavior. God then graced me with the gift of being able to admit that I cannot do this alone. I need God's help and the help of other food addicts in the FAA fellowship.

I am grateful to have an FAA meeting to go to; it has made all the difference in my life. I am grateful that I have been led to our fellowship and that I am living life abstinently.

For today, I am grateful to know that I am a food addict and pray for the grace to accept the gift of unconditional abstinence.

New Year's Eve

Today I celebrate the approaching New Year with a clear mind, body, and soul.

I recall those New Year's Eves of the past. I would eat until the clock struck midnight, resolving to begin a diet the next day. I was certain that *this* year I would finally transform into a slim and happy version of myself.

Numbers had a lot of power when I was in active addiction. I calculated calories consumed and burned, and I estimated and continually revised projected weight loss for two, four, or six months down the line. The number on the scale determined my self-esteem and could make or break my mood on any given day. The last day of each month was a last chance to indulge. Each month's new beginning carried the illusory hope of a new diet, as did each holiday, birthday, and astronomical event, such as a new moon or the summer solstice. With each New Year, of course, I projected dreams of real and lasting change.

What a breath of fresh air it is to celebrate this New Year's Eve, not with intentions of leaving my old self behind, but rather of continuing steadily along this intriguing spiritual journey of recovery.

For today, I ask God to keep me centered, serene, and abstinent as I anticipate the dawning of the New Year.

The Twelve Steps

1. We admitted we were powerless over our food addiction – that our lives had become unmanageable.
2. Came to believe that a Power greater than ourselves could restore us to sanity.
3. Made a decision to turn our will and our lives over to the care of God as we understood God.
4. Made a searching and fearless moral inventory of ourselves.
5. Admitted to God, to ourselves, and to another human being the exact nature of our wrongs.
6. Were entirely ready to have God remove all these defects of character.
7. Humbly asked God to remove our shortcomings.
8. Made a list of all persons we had harmed and became willing to make amends to them all.
9. Made direct amends to such people wherever possible, except when to do so would injure them or others.
10. Continued to take personal inventory and when we were wrong promptly admitted it.
11. Sought through prayer and meditation to improve our conscious contact with God as we understood God, praying only for knowledge of God's will for us and the power to carry that out.
12. Having had a spiritual awakening as the result of these steps, we tried to carry this message to food addicts, and to practice these principles in all our affairs.

The Twelve Traditions

1. Our common welfare should come first; personal recovery depends on FAA unity.
2. For our group purpose there is but one ultimate authority – a loving God as God is expressed in our group conscience. Our leaders are but trusted servants; they do not govern.
3. The only requirement for FAA membership is a desire to stop eating addictive foods.
4. Each group should be autonomous except in matters affecting other groups or FAA as a whole.
5. Each group has but one primary purpose – to carry its message to the food addict who still suffers.
6. An FAA group ought never endorse, finance or lend the FAA name to any related facility or outside enterprise, lest problems of money, property, or prestige divert us from our primary purpose.
7. Every FAA group ought to be fully self-supporting, declining outside contributions.
8. Food Addicts Anonymous should remain forever nonprofessional, but our service centers may employ special workers.
9. FAA, as such, ought never be organized; but we may create service boards or committees directly responsible to those they serve.
10. Food Addicts Anonymous has no opinions on outside issues; hence the FAA name ought never be drawn into public controversy.
11. Our public relations policy is based on attraction rather than promotion; we need always maintain personal anonymity at the level of press, radio and films.
12. Anonymity is the spiritual foundation of all our traditions, ever reminding us to place principles before personalities.

The Promises

1. We will know freedom and the promises of a happy and healthy life.
2. Our creativity will flow with the self-discipline we need to put it into action.
3. The chaos inside us will be gone, so the chaos around us will diminish.
4. Our thinking will become clear.
5. We will be able to learn new information and knowledge and retain what we have learned.
6. We will accomplish complicated tasks with less confusion than before we were abstinent.
7. We will be consistent and dependable.
8. We will no longer fear trying something new and different.
9. If an endeavor is unsuccessful, we will be able to regroup and try it a new way.
10. We will be able to listen to others' ideas and suggestions without becoming defensive or argumentative.
11. We will become present and alert around our friends, family, and significant others.
12. We won't have to shut down, dissociate, or avoid listening any more.
13. We can be ourselves because we won't allow abuse of any kind to be done to us by ourselves or others.
14. We will no longer attempt to fill our emotional and spiritual needs through our mouths. Instead, we will use our mouths along with our hearts to ask for what we need and deserve as children of God.

The Promises

15. We will be able to listen with empathy to others' suffering.
16. We will not need to be controlling or insistent that "our way is best."
17. We will no longer be judgmental about everyone we meet.
18. The urge to see all the ways we were less sick than others will leave us.
19. Our self-esteem will no longer be tangled up in our perceptions about our bodies.
20. If on any given day we think we look fat, ugly or old, we can choose not to lash out in anger or frustration at the people around us.
21. We will be able to hear and feel our Higher Power in our hearts and be still.
22. We will no longer experience the panic, fear, and anxiety of our yesterdays.
23. When presented with multiple choices, we will be able to reach clear decisions and understand what is appropriate for us.
24. We will know freedom from the fear of change in our relationships with the community, our families, and our friends.
25. We will begin to trust our intuition.
26. We will cherish our abstinence as critical to our physical, emotional, and spiritual survival, and we will stay abstinent!

C

Celebrate: 45, 186, 360
Challenges: 200, 296
Change: 78, 121, 214, 217, 248, 253, 260, 277, 324
Character Defects: 122, 147, 156, 161, 164, 193
Choice: 35, 104, 125, 208, 251, 349, 351, 357
Clarity: 121, 125, 149, 158, 205, 237, 287, 288, 307, 327, 334, 343
Commitment: 108, 226, 281, 351
Compare: 79, 266
Compassion: 148, 256
Complacency: 189
Consequences: 157
Control: 72, 163, 224, 285, 304, 358
Courage: 38, 244
Cravings: 103, 117, 195, 220, 346

D

Denial: 30, 70, 74, 77, 83, 131, 156, 203, 238, 259, 264, 278, 299, 305, 364, 365
Desire: 18, 23, 218
Diet Mentality: 100, 225, 283, 300
Differences: 199
Direction: 247, 259
Dishonesty: 230, 305

E

Ego Deflation: 30, 43
Emotions: 41, 94, 99, 134, 155, 258
Empathy: 175, 209
Exercise: 81, 100, 181
Experience: 63, 203

F

Faith: 58, 61, 107, 211, 219, 273, 279, 338, 358
Fear: 10, 83, 109, 111, 113, 119, 151, 153, 211, 266, 358
Feelings: 98, 260, 261, 322, 353, 357
Fellowship: 37, 64, 78, 150, 206, 313, 318, 321, 329, 344, 365
Food Plan: 71, 210, 251, 283
Footwork: 16, 66, 301
Forgiveness: 229, 243
Foundation: 312, 362
Freedom: 7, 21, 26, 31, 40, 83, 96, 97,123, 133, 140, 149, 153, 205, 234, 298, 315, 319, 360

G

Gifts of Recovery: 188, 197, 233, 295, 355
Going to Any Lengths: 207, 281, 362
Gratification: 49, 157
Gratitude: 6, 7, 18, 50, 51, 76, 87, 124, 135, 146, 154, 219, 223, 234, 250, 267, 296, 305, 323, 342, 351
Guidance: 6, 32, 44, 293, 313, 333

M

N

O

P

STEPS: